# Your Shirt Is Not an Oven Mitt!

Also by Debbie Puente

*Elegantly Easy Liqueur Desserts & Crème Brûlée*

*Elegantly Easy Crème Brûlée & Other Custard Desserts*

*Deceptively Simple*

# Your Shirt Is Not an Oven Mitt!

A KITCHEN SURVIVAL MANUAL WITH
150+ FOOLPROOF RECIPES

Debbie Puente

St. Martin's Griffin
New York

www.stmartins.com

BOOK DESIGN BY AMANDA DEWEY
ILLUSTRATIONS BY DOMINGO NUÑO

Library of Congress Cataloging-in-Publication Data

Puente, Debbie.
    Your shirt is not an oven mitt! : a kitchen survival manual with 150+ foolproof recipes / Debbie Puente.—1st St. Martin's Griffin ed.
        p. cm.
    ISBN 0-312-33124-X
    EAN 978-0312-33124-5
    1. Cookery.   I. Title.
    TX714.P84 2004
    641.5—dc22

                                                            2004002741

First Edition: August 2004

10   9   8   7   6   5   4   3   2   1

*To Evelyn, my mother,*
*and*
*to Sheldon, my dad,*
*for a million reasons, but most of all*
*for always making me feel loved*

# Contents

# Acknowledgments

No book is ever written without help, and I have some people to thank: First, **Evelyn Howard**, my mother, who does about 70 percent of my grocery shopping. While I can't say that my mom taught me how to cook, I can say that she taught me how to shop. Mom, I love you so much! My father and stepmom, **Sheldon** and **Barbara Howard**, have the very best eyes when it comes to my grammar, and nothing I write goes out without a once-over from them, not even this ac-knowledgment. My husband, **David**, and sons, **Joey, Steven**, and **Cole**, are my guys, from whom I am so fortunate to have such love and support. It's David who sees to it that the boys never feel neglected when I'm deep into writing. He always picks up the slack at mealtimes. Thanks to my beloved mother-in-law, **Ralphie Puente**, and my sisters, **Iris, Judi, Beth**, and **Jo**—you all make me feel so loved and encouraged. Always. Thanks to my manager, **Heidi Rotbart**, and lawyer, **Leslie Abell**, for always watching my back. Thanks also go to **Marie Estrada**, the patient editor of this book, for all her hard work putting this together, and

**Suzanne Fass** for the tedious task of copyediting—you did a fantastic job. To everyone on the New York production team at St. Martin's Press, I offer heartfelt thanks. To **Jerilyn Dufresne**, my thanks for her help with the editing; to the **Housewife Writers** for always having the best advice; and to my **Coffee Girls** (also at times known as my Lemon Drop Girls), my companions and friends over these many years, life is just more fun because of you.

# Introduction

Are you a culinary klutz? A kitchen novice? A recent graduate, newly married, or a single bachelor who wants to expand his repertoire of recipes beyond "the one *nothing fancy* dish I make"?

I've designed *Your Shirt Is Not an Oven Mitt!* with you in mind. Featuring a combination of hints and tips, handy lists, and more than 150 delicious, easy-to-follow, basic-ingredient recipes that are also cost conscious and nutritious, *Your Shirt Is Not an Oven Mitt!* is the only guide you'll need.

You really can cook. (Cooking isn't rocket science, but it is a science.) How does Chile Relleno Casserole sound? No one will believe that it only took you minutes to prepare. Nutty Caramel Cinnamon Buns? Your friends will declare you an instant success, that is, if you can get yourself to share such creations with others.

The average recipe in *Your Shirt Is Not an Oven Mitt!* will provide a feast for you or a generous meal for two with plenty of leftovers—for less than the cost of one super-sized fast-food meal. However, I realize that nutritional needs vary. A college athlete will need a lot more fuel than a computer programmer; therefore, the number of servings are only estimates. Also, feel free to substitute any kind of chicken parts for chicken breasts. Add your favorite herbs and spices to any dish—after all, seasoning is personal. If a certain fruit is not in season, substitute one that is. If you really love cheese, use more than the recipe calls for. However, when baking—breads, cakes, cookies, etc.—accurate measuring is required.

*veggie*

Take note of the three icons on this page, symbols you'll see throughout. I know many of you are vegetarians, or have at least one friend who is. So not only have I included meatless recipes that will please even the staunchest carnivore, but the icon shows where vegetarian substitutes can easily be made. Many recipes, in addition to those in the Microwave Marvels chapter, can be adapted for the microwave. Just look for the Zap It symbol.

Gadgets can make your culinary world more convenient. A rice cooker, for example, doubles as the perfect slow-cooked oatmeal maker. Look for the gadget icon. Perhaps the next time a birthday rolls around, or when you're ready for a new household purchase, consider a rice cooker, slow cooker, waffle maker, fondue pot, or best of all, a juicer!

And remember: You really can cook!

# Your Shirt Is Not an Oven Mitt!

# 1.

# Your Shirt Is Not an Oven Mitt! Safety First

## AVOID GETTING BURNED, CUT, OR ELECTROCUTED

The kitchen can be a hazardous place where so many things could go wrong. Be cautious and prepared. You can avoid getting burned, cut, or electrocuted in the kitchen—things that put a damper on any dinner party—by following some basic safety rules.

- Take your time. Accidents happen when you become frustrated or when you're in too much of a hurry. Three-minute eggs become an all-night affair when you're delayed in the emergency room.
- Keep pot holders and oven mitts dry. Damp pot holders will transfer heat from the pan right to your hand. Also, when buying pot holders, look for thick, well-insulated, heavy-duty oven mitts that cover your entire hand plus part of your forearm.

- Lift lids away from your face when peeking into a pot. Steam is very hot and can be completely invisible.
- Make sure the long handles of pots and pans are away from foot traffic. Turn them to the back or center of the stove.
- Roll up your sleeves. The singed and blistered look is never in.
- Don't use the toaster, blender, or other appliances near the kitchen sink. You could receive an electric shock and be seriously injured if water touches electric appliances.
- Keep a small fire extinguisher, or at least a box of baking soda, within reach of your cooking area. It's impossible to blow out a grease fire. And never use water on a cooking fire or an electric appliance—that may result in an explosion. If something you're broiling happens to catch fire, do not pour water on it. Shut the oven door and immediately turn off the broiler. Most broiler fires will suffocate themselves; if the fire persists, however, use a fire extinguisher.
- Never plug or unplug appliances with wet hands. Or any other wet body part.
- Always cut on a proper cutting surface. Placing a damp towel under a cutting board will keep it from sliding around. Or use cutting boards with rubber, non-skid feet.
- Keep your knives sharp. Dull knives can slip and end up cutting you because you'll use more pressure to cut.
- Immediately dispose of aluminum cans and sharp lids. I have a few scars to remind me of how important it is to dispose of that jagged lid properly.
- Never put a utensil or your hand inside a working blender or mixer.

## FOOD POISONING AND OTHER FOOD-BORNE ILLNESSES

Nothing impresses a potential date less than throwing up. With that in mind, you may want to consider these hints to avoid food poisoning and other food-borne illnesses.

### *While grocery shopping:*
- Don't let juices from raw meat, poultry, or fish drip onto your hands or on any fresh produce in your grocery cart. Raw juices contain bacteria. Use the plastic bags offered at the counter.
- Shop for cold and frozen products last. Use a cooler for the ride home, especially during the summer or if you're running other errands.

*In the kitchen:*

- Avoid foods made with raw eggs. Older cookbooks may have recipes for ice cream, mayonnaise, eggnog, and some desserts that call for raw eggs. We do not recommend following these recipes because of the risk of salmonella. The commercial versions of these products are made with pasteurized eggs (eggs that have been sufficiently heated to kill bacteria) and are not a food hazard. Remember: this means no sampling of cake batters and cookie dough before they are baked! For more on egg safety, see the **Eggs Aren't Just for Breakfast** chapter and the section on eggs in the Food Storage Index.
- Always wash your hands in hot, soapy water before and after handling raw meat, poultry, seafood, or eggs.
- Sanitize your dishcloths or sponges on a regular basis, or use disposable cloths. A contaminated dishcloth can house millions of bacteria within a few hours. Consider using paper towels to clean up, and throw them away immediately.
- Keep your can opener clean.
- Wash your cutting board with soap and hot water after each use. Which is safer to use, wood or plastic? In 1997, University of Wisconsin food scientists shocked the world when they announced that bacteria thrive on plastic but are mysteriously killed on wooden cutting boards. No one has been able to duplicate these findings. In fact, new studies by the Food and Drug Administration (FDA) show that bacteria become trapped in wooden cutting boards and are difficult to dislodge by rinsing. U.S. Department of Agriculture (USDA) researchers have found that raw meat leaves fewer bacteria on plastic than on wood boards, and it's easier to wash bacteria off plastic boards. If you do purchase a wooden cutting board, I recommend using mineral oil to season it. Mineral oil is tasteless and odorless and will never become rancid or sticky. Here's how to do it: rub a few tablespoons of oil on the wood, allowing it to soak in. Repeat the process the next few days, or until the oil is no longer being absorbed. Wipe off any excess that remains on the surface. Always remember to dry wooden boards thoroughly after washing.
- Cook all meat and poultry—or casseroles that contain meat or poultry—at a minimum oven temperature of 325°F. Cook meats thoroughly, but don't overcook them. Heat kills bacteria, but too much heat causes meat, poultry, and fish to form possibly carcinogenic compounds. Use a meat thermometer in the thickest part of the meat, avoiding the bone. A thermometer should never be inserted into meat that has not yet been seared;

the thermometer can transfer bacteria from the exterior into the interior. According to the USDA, meat should be cooked at least to these internal temperatures: beef, lamb, or veal roasts, steaks, and chops: 145°F; ground beef, pork, lamb, or veal: 160°F; ground chicken or turkey or stuffing: 165°F; poultry: 180°F.

- Keep your refrigerator at or below 40°F, and your freezer at 0°F. Food kept continuously frozen at 0°F will always be safe but the quality suffers with lengthy freezer storage. Food is properly refrigerated at a temperature range between 35° to 40°F or 2° to 6°C. A temperature of 40°F or colder slows the growth of most bacteria. The fewer bacteria there are, the less likely you are to get sick. Date leftovers so they can be used within two to three days. If in doubt, throw it out! There's no such thing as homemade penicillin.

- Store uncooked food below cooked food in the refrigerator to avoid contamination from drippings. (Or better yet, keep everything in well-sealed containers to eliminate the possibility of dripping.)

- Marinate raw meat and poultry in the refrigerator, not on the counter. Don't serve the marinade unless you've boiled it at least one minute. And don't baste your food with uncooked marinade.

- Don't store raw fish in your refrigerator for more than 24 hours. Raw poultry or ground beef will keep for one to two days; raw red meat will keep for three to five days.

- Never thaw frozen food at room temperature. Thaw meat, poultry, and fish products in the refrigerator, microwave oven, or cold water that you change every 30 minutes. Changing the water every 30 minutes ensures that the food is kept cold, an important factor in slowing bacterial growth on the outside while the inside is still thawing.

- Cook microwave-thawed food immediately after thawing.

- Never put cooked food on the same plate that was used for raw food unless the plate has been thoroughly washed.

## CUTS AND BURNS

- If you cut yourself, immediately wash the area with antiseptic and apply pressure with a clean towel. If the cut is not too deep and the bleeding stops, apply an antiseptic cream and bandage. However, if the cut is deep and there is heavy bleeding, apply direct pressure and seek medical help.

- If you burn yourself by touching something hot, immediately apply an ice pack or submerge your hand in ice water. If the ice water becomes too uncomfortable, remove your hand until the pain begins to return; keep repeating until the pain subsides. If the burning pain lasts more than an hour, call a doctor. Do not apply a burn cream until after the burning sensation is gone. A first-degree burn will turn red. A second-degree burn will blister. For anything more serious, you need to seek medical help.

## BASIC KITCHEN CHEMISTRY AND COMMONLY ASKED QUESTIONS

Cooks use many of the same methods in the kitchen as chemists use in the lab: measuring and combining ingredients, heating, cooling, shaking, and stirring. And both, on more than one documented occasion, have created concoctions capable of wiping out society as we know it. Many common cooking ingredients such as salt, sugar, baking soda, and baking powder, if measured or combined incorrectly with other ingredients, will cause the recipe to fail.

Before you begin any recipe, read the recipe carefully to be sure you will have the right ingredients.

### What is the difference between baking soda and baking powder?

Over the years, it has been my experience that this is the most common question a new cook asks. Both ingredients enable the batters of cakes, cookies, muffins, and biscuits to rise. However, batters containing acidic liquid ingredients such as citrus juice, buttermilk, yogurt, sour cream, or vinegar, need baking soda to neutralize the acid and release carbon dioxide gas. The gas is trapped as bubbles in the batter, expanding in the heat of an oven. If the batter doesn't contain much acid, the recipe will call for baking powder. Baking powder is actually baking soda with acid added; it needs liquid and heat to release its carbon dioxide gas.

### Why is gravy so lumpy sometimes?

You can have smooth gravy every time if you know the trick. Starch makes gravy thick. Common starches used in cooking are cornstarch, potato starch, and flour. If starch is added directly to hot liquid, starch granules form which are sticky on the outside but dry on the inside, lump together, and don't dissolve into the liquid. In contrast, adding starch to cold liquid allows the granules to evenly disperse, soak up the liquid, and swell like sponges. The longer the liquid is heated, the thicker and creamier it gets. So chances are, the last time you had lumpy gravy, it was because Grandma added flour directly into her hot liquid. Next time, why don't you offer to help Grandma make the gravy? In a small bowl, mix a few tablespoons of flour with a cold liquid. When the flour is completely dissolved, pour the mixture into the hot liquid. Cook over low heat, stirring constantly, until the mixture comes to a boil. Reduce the heat and keep warm until ready to serve. And always remember to point out how utterly smooth your gravy is.

### How do I avoid tears when chopping onions?

This is a cinch when you discover *why* onions make you cry. When you cut an onion, you're actually cutting through cells and releasing sulphur-containing molecules. These molecules form sulfuric acid when they react with the tears in your eyes, causing the burning sensation. If the sulphur molecules are given another moisture source to react with before they reach your eyes, you can avoid the tears and stinging. When you cut an onion, do it very close to, or directly under, cold running water. Another trick is to put the onion in the freezer for 10 minutes before you cut it. The low temperature will slow the formation of the burning molecules. This trick may not work for the extremely sensitive, so I offer one foolproof tip: wear safety goggles.

### Have ice crystals formed in your ice cream?

If your ice cream makes too many long trips between the freezer, the counter, and back to the freezer again, it will most likely form an icy and grainy texture. Every time the ice cream begins to melt, the water content separates from the fat content. When the ice cream is frozen again, the water, now separated from the fat, reforms into large ice crystals. If you accidentally leave your ice cream out long enough to cause severe melting, simply blend it up, return it to its container, and refreeze.

### What about quick fixes?

Many people use candy bars, or the so-called sports bar, for a quick pick-me-up. These bars do provide a quick energy boost because sugar is digested and absorbed quickly. But there are better choices. These bars may help take away that lethargy due to a lack of food, but for a fraction of the price, so will a few graham crackers with milk or juice, granola bars, bananas, oranges, and bagels.

Yes, hot chicken soup really does help when you have a cold. And so will hot tea. It's all in the heat. When you have a cold, your respiratory tract becomes congested. The heat helps to clear congestion and aid in breathing. A tasty chicken soup also provides comfort and good nutrition.

# 2.

# Saving Money,
# Saving Time

## BECOMING A SMARTER COOK

Relax. You're smart enough. Recipes are only guidelines, so have fun. You'll make mistakes, but you'll learn from them. This chapter will help you to organize your kitchen, plan meals, manage grocery costs, and lots more.

*At the market:*
- Don't shop while hungry.
- Shop with a list to avoid impulse buying. Keep your list handy—on the refrigerator with a magnet works great—and write on it the moment you realize you need something. Don't wait until just before you're running out the door to start your list.
- Keep a week-to-week price list until you become familiar with regular food prices. Then you will be able to decide which specials are good deals.

- Use coupons for items you repeatedly buy.
- For storing foods, choose the best, low-cost wrapping material. Wax paper often performs the same function at lower cost than foil or plastic wrap. Also save reusable containers for storing foods in the refrigerator or freezer.
- Buy fresh fruits and vegetables in season, when the abundance is the greatest and the price is the lowest. Eat asparagus in the spring, nectarines in summer, apples in fall, and oranges in the winter.
- Avoid ready-made or ready-to-bake cakes and cookies, canned soft drinks, and most convenience foods. A can of soda can cost as much as one dollar, but a glass of iced tea costs only a few cents. A glass of orange juice is about fifteen cents. Cookies can cost up to seven dollars per pound, but a homemade sugar cookie is about a penny. Frozen dinners are not only overpriced, but they're also overcooked (and over- just about everything, including salt and fat). A simple rule of thumb . . . if it's easy, it's overpriced.
- If your market doesn't have a butcher counter, ring the bell for service and request just one-quarter pound of ground beef or one chicken breast. Don't purchase larger prepackaged foods if you only want small portions. Larger sizes are false economy if you end up with leftovers that get trashed after a few days.
- If your market does have a butcher, get on friendly terms with him or her. You might be surprised how happy your butcher is to answer questions you may have and help you out.
- Try something new and unfamiliar every time you visit the produce section, and expand your horizons. Buy half a pound of some vegetable you've never tried before, take it home, steam it, melt a little butter on it, and maybe you will love it! It certainly can't hurt you.
- Avoid shopping for food in convenience stores and delis. They are good in a pinch but expensive.
- Planning ahead will help you to eat more nutritiously and save you money. Always keep the common food staples on hand, and keep as much as space allows. (See the lists on the pages that follow for helpful tips.)
- Try "alternative shopping." Explore your local Asian or Middle Eastern grocery store. Visit the local farmers' market and health or natural foods market.

*At home:*

- Read recipes carefully before you begin. Are there any steps you should be doing first, such as beating eggs, chopping onions, melting butter?
- Assemble all ingredients and utensils before beginning your recipe. There's nothing more frustrating than finding out halfway through making your Cherries Jubilee that it is just going to be Jubilee.
- Preheat the oven. Check the recipe for the proper time to turn on the oven. Many recipes call for preheating the oven while you prep the recipe so it will reach the correct temperature by the time the food is ready to be baked.
- Clean as you go to avoid a big, overwhelming mess. Or you could always invite your Type A neat-freak friend to dinner and let him or her go wild in your kitchen.
- If you're hesitant or anxious about using a sharp knife, try a good pair of kitchen shears instead. They can be used for a variety of kitchen jobs, such as snipping herbs and cutting up a whole chicken.
- As long as you're chopping something (onions, celery, green peppers, etc.) go ahead and chop extra. Store in sandwich bags in the refrigerator until you need them the next time.
- If you have access to a large oven, about once a month or so get a few friends together and make a turkey. Turkey is one of the great meat bargains available. Out of a 16-pound turkey, you should be able to get the equivalent of 24 servings. See page 128 for how to do it. After the initial feast, divide up the leftovers to use in sandwiches, salads, and soups. Using the turkey this way comes out to an average of forty cents a serving.
- Learn to love beans. They're cheap, very low in fat, and nutritious.
- Stretch your more expensive meat dishes by serving them inside baked potatoes, on top of rice, or as filling inside a tortilla or pita.

# BASIC PANTRY ITEMS AND STAPLES YOU SHOULD ALWAYS HAVE ON HAND

## SHELF LIST

Some of these items should be refrigerated after opening; check the label. Also, see the **Food Storage Index** located at the back of the book.

PEANUT BUTTER

JUST-ADD-WATER PANCAKE MIX

QUICK-COOKING OATMEAL AND OTHER CEREALS

GRANULATED WHITE SUGAR

BROWN SUGAR (light or dark)

POTATOES

RICE

DRIED AND CANNED BEANS

CANNED CHICKEN BROTH

CANNED "CREAM OF" SOUPS

ONIONS

GARLIC

ALL-PURPOSE FLOUR

SALT

BLACK PEPPER

BAKING SODA

BAKING POWDER

COFFEE AND TEA

VEGETABLE SHORTENING

HERBS AND SPICES (cumin, oregano, basil, ground cinnamon, ground ginger)

CAJUN SEASONING MIX

BOTTLED SALAD DRESSINGS

OLIVE OR OTHER VEGETABLE OILS

SOY SAUCE

HONEY

CANNED TUNA

DRIED FRUIT

RAMEN

DRIED PASTAS

PRETZELS

MUSTARD

WORCESTERSHIRE SAUCE

KETCHUP

BREAD, ROLLS, TORTILLAS, PITA

FRUIT AND/OR VEGETABLE JUICES

PANCAKE SYRUP

CANNED AND/OR JARRED SOUP

JAM AND/OR JELLY

DRY DRINK MIXES (hot cocoa, instant breakfast)

PROTEIN BARS

PROTEIN POWDER

## REFRIGERATOR LIST

| | |
|---|---|
| EGGS | TOFU |
| MILK | FRUITS, VEGETABLES |
| CHEESE | SALAD GREENS |
| BUTTER, MARGARINE | YOGURT |
| MAYONNAISE | WHEAT GERM |

## NOT-SO-BASIC BASICS

Store these items according to the label's storing instructions.

| | |
|---|---|
| SESAME SEEDS | VANILLA EXTRACT |
| TAHINI | CHOCOLATE CHIPS |
| ROASTED PEPPERS | MARSHMALLOW FLUFF |
| SUN-DRIED TOMATOES | HEAVY CREAM |
| MARINATED ARTICHOKES | PESTO SAUCES |
| PIMENTOS | CURRY POWDER |

## BASIC KITCHEN EQUIPMENT

Unless you have an endless supply of money, I highly recommend shopping for the following items at yard sales, resale shops, and discount stores. You may first want to visit a good retail kitchen-supply store to familiarize yourself with what brands are high quality. Choose the right pan for what you like to cook, and how you like to cook. Before you shop for cooking equipment, analyze your lifestyle and your tolerance for scrubbing. If I had to take just one pot or pan with me on a camping trip, it would be my 10-inch nonstick Mirro frying pan that I purchased in a pancake emergency while on a ski trip. It was less than $20 at the local hardware store, and I use it more than the fancy pan that happens to be ten times the price. The only disadvantage of nonstick cookware is that you can't use metal utensils. However, you don't need metal because the new plastic utensils are designed to handle very high temperatures. On the other hand, if you share a kitchen with others, and can't trust them to handle your non-stick cookware with care, you should purchase an abuse-proof pan made from hard-anodized aluminum (Calphalon). Yes, they're expensive, but you'll never have to replace them.

## COOKWARE AND ELECTRICS

8- OR 10-INCH SKILLET OR FRYING PAN

COVERED SAUCEPANS (2-, 4-, and 6-quart)

OVENPROOF AND/OR MICROWAVE-SAFE
CASSEROLES AND BAKING DISHES
(2-, 3-, and 4-quart)

MULTIPURPOSE ROASTING PAN WITH
NONSTICK RACK

TOASTER OVEN (not pop-up)

BLENDER

JUICER

## TOOLS

CAN AND BOTTLE OPENER

GRATER OR SHREDDER

PANCAKE TURNER
(flat heat-proof plastic spatula)

VEGETABLE PEELER

KITCHEN SHEARS

TONGS

PARING KNIFE

BUTTER KNIFE

SERRATED KNIFE

STRAINER AND/OR COLANDER

LONG-HANDLED WOODEN SPOON

DINNER PLATES (at least two)

CEREAL/SOUP BOWLS (at least two)

EATING UTENSILS

CLOTHESPINS (for sealing chip
and snack bags)

DISH SOAP AND SPONGE/SCRUBBIE

CUTTING BOARD

## For Measuring, Mixing, and Baking

SET OF MEASURING CUPS

MEASURING SPOONS

ROTARY BEATER

WAX PAPER

WIRE WHISK

MIXING BOWLS—SMALL, MEDIUM, LARGE

MICROWAVABLE CONTAINERS

RUBBER SPATULA

COOKIE SHEETS

POT HOLDERS, HOT PADS

## Other

COOKBOOKS—GO FOR THE ALL-PURPOSE
STYLE COOKBOOKS WITH LOTS
OF PRACTICAL RECIPES AND KITCHEN TIPS

WINE BOTTLE OPENER

BROWN LUNCH BAGS

ZIPPER-LOCK PLASTIC SANDWICH BAGS
OR PLASTIC WRAP

FOIL

THERMOS BOTTLES

NONSTICK GRIDDLE

# 3.

# Eggs Aren't Just for Breakfast

Eggs are a wonderful source of nutrition, and also a terrific value. One serving of two eggs is fairly standard breakfast fare, and costs, on average, about twenty-five cents. Eggs are also quite versatile. Eggs can be fried, scrambled, boiled, poached, and added to other dishes (such as fried rice and ramen) to bump up the protein and make the dish more substantial. Always store eggs in the refrigerator. When shopping for eggs, check the date and buy the freshest and largest. Generally, larger eggs are more economical and are almost always called for in recipes.

The color of the eggshell is an indication of the breed of the hen and has nothing to do with the quality of the egg, its flavor, or nutritional value. The color of the egg yolk does depend on the hen's diet: hens fed on yellow corn lay eggs with lighter yolks than wheat-fed hens. The shell protects the egg and if it is cracked or damaged, the contents will deteriorate rapidly; eggs with cracked shells should not be used. Always buy eggs from the refrigerated dairy case rather than from a room-temperature display. (Eggs stored at room temperature lose more quality in one day than in a week in the refrigerator.) As mentioned in Chapter One, avoid foods made with raw eggs. When eggs are cooked to a temperature of 140°F, all harmful bacteria will be killed. Egg whites firm up and set at 145°F and yolks thicken and set at 156°F. Eggs are safe when the white is set and the yolk is just starting to firm, which means that you can still enjoy your eggs soft and moist.

There are recipes that incorporate eggs throughout this book. See the index for a complete listing.

"The chance of encountering an egg contaminated with Salmonella Enteritidis (SE) is very small and the possibility of becoming ill from SE can be eliminated completely with proper handling and cooking," according to Jill Snowdon, PhD, director of food safety for the American Egg Board's Egg Nutrition Center. Based on calculations from the 1998 USDA Salmonella Risk Assessment Report, one egg per 20,000 is contaminated with SE (.005%).

According to John Mason, DVM, MPH, the former director of the USDA Salmonella Enteritidis Control Program, "Based on USDA's statistics, the average consumer would encounter a contaminated egg only once in forty-two years. And then, that egg would have to be time-and-temperature abused to contribute to a health problem." The risk of contracting egg-related Salmonella is extremely low for healthy individuals, according to Dr. Mason. "There is one outbreak for every one billion eggs consumed," he said.

According to statistics from the Centers for Disease Control (CDC), the number of Salmonella Enteritidis outbreaks (two or more people) has steadily declined from a high of seventy-seven in 1989 to forty-four in 1997. Outbreaks linked to shell eggs have steadily declined to a low of seventeen in 1997. Additionally, there has been a 44% decrease in the incidence of Salmonella Enteritidis from eggs in the last three years, according to 1998 FoodNet system for surveillance.

The egg industry makes every effort to ensure that consumers receive the safest, highest-quality product possible, and is proactively involved in minimizing the risk of egg-related Salmonella through various food safety initiatives. These include quality-assurance programs, educational programs, and research funding.

*Source: Egg Nutrition Center*


## EGG SAFETY TIPS:

- Refrigeration is the first step in proper egg handling. Keep shell eggs, broken-out eggs, or egg mixtures refrigerated before and after cooking.

- Do not leave eggs in any form at room temperature for more than 2 hours, including preparation and serving.
- Promptly after serving, refrigerate leftovers in shallow containers so they will cool quickly.
- Cleanliness of hands, utensils, and work surfaces is essential.
- Use only unbroken eggs. Discard cracked eggs and avoid mixing the shell with the egg's contents. But just in case, play it safe. Break eggs one-by-one to prevent one bad one from ruining the others.

## THINGS YOU NEED TO KNOW ABOUT HARD- AND SOFT-BOILED EGGS

Preparing hard- and soft-boiled eggs is simple, yes, but it still requires a little practice to achieve excellence. For starters, the term "boiled eggs" is somewhat deceptive. Eggs should never be boiled; they should be cooked gently at no more than a simmer. Boiling eggs at high heat will overcook the egg, leaving the whites tough and rubbery. Also, boiling water will toss the eggs all around, leaving the shells cracked and causing them to leak. You may wonder what the best way is to peel a hard-boiled egg—the fresher the egg, the harder to peel; the older the egg, the larger the air cell, and the easier to peel. Chilling hard-boiled eggs allows the white to firm and makes peeling easier. Also, holding an egg under a stream of cold water as you peel removes any bits of broken shell.

If you're not planning on eating your hard-boiled eggs right away, it is best to keep them stored in their shells in the refrigerator, where they will be good for one week. A hard-boiled egg out of its shell should be stored, tightly sealed, in the refrigerator for no more than one week. If you have forgotten whether an egg is hard-boiled or raw, set it on a countertop and give it a spin. A hard-boiled egg will spin evenly like a top, while a raw egg will move unsteadily and tumble around as the yolk sloshes around inside. Some cooks add a drop or two of food coloring to the simmering water to tint the shells of the hard-boiled eggs, to make them instantly recognizable and set them apart from the raw eggs. Another alternative is to simply mark them with a pencil or pen.

# Hard-Boiled Eggs

*Serves 1 or 2*

**Water**

**2 to 4 eggs**

Be sure the saucepan you are using is large enough to hold the eggs in a single layer. Bring the water to a boil over high heat. Gently lower the eggs into the water with a large slotted spoon, solid spoon, or a strainer. Reduce the heat to low and simmer the eggs for 15 minutes. Cool the eggs by removing from the heat, and running them under cold water. I find it easiest to gently pour the hot water and eggs into a large colander or strainer, set the hot pan aside to cool, and plunge the eggs into a bowl of cold water.

# Soft-Boiled Eggs

*Serves 1 or 2*

Perfect food to have when the tummy is a little queazy.

**Water**

**2 to 4 eggs**

Prepare as for Hard-Boiled Eggs, allowing 3 minutes for very soft eggs. For slightly firmer yet still soft eggs, cook for 4 minutes. Remove and serve immediately.

# Deviled Eggs

*Serves 2 or 3*

Perfect for entertaining!

*6 hard-boiled eggs, peeled*
*1 teaspoon prepared mustard*
*3 tablespoons mayonnaise*
*1 teaspoon rice vinegar or other mild vinegar*
*¼ teaspoon Worcestershire sauce*
*Salt and pepper*
*Paprika, optional*
*Zipper-lock sandwich bag*

Slice each egg in half lengthwise. Remove yolks and place in a medium bowl. Arrange whites on a serving platter. Mash yolks with a fork until no large lumps are left. Add mustard, mayonnaise, vinegar, worcestershire, and salt and pepper, and mix with a rubber spatula, mashing mixture against the side of the bowl until smooth. Fill a zipper-lock bag with yolk mixture. Snip off one corner and gently pipe yolk into egg white halves. Sprinkle with paprika, if desired.

# Fluffy Soft Scrambled Eggs

*Serves 1 or 2*

The trick is not to overcook!

*4 large eggs*
*Salt and pepper*
*¼ cup milk*
*1 to 2 teaspoons butter*
*Hot sauce*

Crack eggs into a large bowl. Add salt and pepper (start with only a pinch, you can always add more) and milk. Whip with a fork until the eggs are blended well. Place butter in a skillet, then place pan over a medium-high heat. When the butter begins to melt, swirl it around and up the side of the pan. Pour in the beaten eggs, and using a wooden spoon or spatula, push the eggs around the pan until they begin to clump together. While the eggs still have a shiny appearance, remove from the heat. Total cooking time should be about 2 minutes. Serve immediately with a dash or two of hot sauce.

# Fried Eggs

*Serves 1 or 2*

**1 tablespoon butter, margarine, bacon fat, or oil**
**2 to 4 eggs**

Melt butter in small skillet over medium heat. Crack eggs directly into the pan. When the whites are completely set and the yolks are nearly set, flip each egg carefully by sliding a flat spatula under the egg, and gently turning it over. Cook for an additional 20 to 30 seconds. For harder yolks, allow the egg to cook for about 1 minute after flipping.

# Fried Eggs over Vegetable-Bacon Hash

*Serves 2*

*1 pound (about 3 medium) potatoes, peeled and cut into ½-inch cubes*
*6 slices bacon, cut into 1-inch pieces*
*1 large red pepper, stemmed, seeded, and cut into ½-inch pieces*
*¼ teaspoon salt*
*1 (15-ounce) can black beans, rinsed and drained*
*4 eggs*

Place potatoes in a large saucepan and add enough water to cover the potatoes. Place over medium-high heat, and bring to a boil. Reduce heat to low; cover and simmer 4 minutes or until potatoes are almost tender. Remove from heat and drain.

In a large nonstick skillet, cook bacon, red pepper, potatoes, and salt over medium-high heat, stirring occasionally with a wood spoon, until vegetables are tender and browned, about 15 minutes. Stir in black beans; heat through.

Cook the eggs according to the Fried Eggs recipe. Serve eggs on top of a generous serving of the hash.

# Circus Eggs

*Serves 1 or 2*

This is actually a variation of the Fried Eggs recipe. My son, Joey, remembers a teacher giving him a version of this recipe in the first grade. It's our favorite way to enjoy eggs.

*2 tablespoons butter or margarine,*
   *plus extra if necessary*
*2 slices bread*
*2 eggs*

Melt the butter in a skillet over medium heat. Cut a hole in each piece of bread. (You can use the lip of a cup for a perfect circle; we just use our fingers.) Place the bread in the pan, cracking 1 egg into each hole. The yolk will fill the hole and the white will be on top of the bread. Cook the egg and bread until the yolk has nearly set. Flip carefully using a flat spatula. Continue cooking for 20 to 30 seconds. Fry the center of the bread (the hole) in the pan as well, adding more butter if needed.

# Fried Rice

And I'll bet you thought it was hard to make.

*2 tablespoons vegetable oil*

*½ cup frozen peas, thawed*

*2 cups cooked rice, cooled*

*2 eggs*

*2 teaspoons soy sauce*

In a large skillet, heat oil over medium-high heat. Add peas. Fry, stirring constantly, for 1 to 2 minutes. Add rice. Stir and fry until hot. Push heated rice mixture to sides of skillet with a wood spoon. Add eggs to center of skillet. Fry, stirring constantly, until eggs are set. Stir cooked eggs and rice mixture together. Season with soy sauce, mixing well.

NOTE: *See page 149 for directions on how to cook rice in the microwave.*

# Cottage Cheese Pancakes

*Serves 1 to 2*

*1 cup small-curd cottage cheese*

*2 tablespoons all-purpose flour*

*2 eggs*

*½ teaspoon salt*

*3 tablespoons butter*

In a medium bowl, using a fork or whisk, mix together the cottage cheese, flour, eggs, and salt. The batter will be lumpy. Melt the butter in a medium skillet over medium-high heat. Drop about 1 heaping tablespoon batter into hot skillet. Cook the pancakes for about 30 seconds on each side, flipping with a flat spatula only once. Serve with fresh fruit.

# Baked Eggs and Spinach

*Serves 2*

1 (10-ounce) package frozen chopped spinach, thawed

1 (3-ounce) package cream cheese, softened

2 eggs

1 cup (4 ounces) shredded Cheddar cheese

Preheat the oven to 400°F. Squeeze out and discard as much liquid from the frozen spinach as possible. Combine the spinach and cream cheese in a blender or small food processor. Don't go overboard; you don't want it too creamy. Fill a small ovenproof baking dish with the spinach. Make a small well with the back of a spoon and carefully break the eggs into it. Cover the eggs with the cheddar cheese. Bake for 20 minutes or until the cheese is melted and crusty.

# Matzo Brei

*Serves 1*

My grandma taught me how to make this when I was only eight years old. Little ones seem to really love it.

*2 pieces of matzo*
*2 eggs, well beaten*
*Salt*
*2 tablespoons butter, margarine, or vegetable oil*

Hold the matzos under hot running water and wet both sides without making them soggy. Place in a colander to drain or place on paper towels. Tear the matzos into small pieces and place in a medium bowl. Add the eggs and stir to coat the matzo pieces. Season with salt. Heat the butter in a skillet and spread the matzo mixture in the pan in a very thin layer, spreading it with a large spoon or spatula. Cook, turning the pieces, until browned and crispy. Serve warm. Goes great with fresh fruit.

# Quiche

*Serves 4*

To go low carb, ditch the pie crust and bake in a buttered pie dish.

    *1 unbaked 9-inch piecrust*
    *2 cups cream, half-and-half, milk, or any combination*
        *of these liquids that adds up to 2 cups*
    *4 eggs*
    *2 to 3 tablespoons finely diced onions or thinly sliced green onions*
    *1 teaspoon salt*
    *1 teaspoon pepper*
    *1 cup (about 12 ounces) Swiss cheese cubes*
        *(think the size of dice)*

Preheat oven to 400°F. Prick piecrust bottom and sides with a fork. Bake on a cookie sheet for 10 to 12 minutes until golden brown. Remove from oven and set aside. Lower oven temperature to 350°F. In a blender, blend the cream, eggs, onions, salt, and pepper. Place cheese into piecrust and slowly pour the cream mixture on top of the cheese. Bake for 30 minutes or until set and no longer liquid. Serve with fresh fruit.

# French Toast

*Serves 1 or 2*

*2 eggs*
*2 slices bread*
*1 tablespoon butter or margarine*
*Powdered sugar*
*Pancake syrup*

In a large shallow bowl, beat the eggs until well combined. Soak the bread in the egg until saturated. Melt the butter in a skillet over medium to medium-low heat. Cook bread until golden brown on one side; turn over with a spatula and cook until second side is golden. Serve with powdered sugar and syrup.

# Pancakes from Scratch

*Serves 2*

1¼ *cup self-rising flour (see Note)*
2 *tablespoons sugar*
1 *cup milk*
1 *egg, beaten*
1 *tablespoon vegetable oil*
*Butter for greasing griddle (optional)*

Preheat a nonstick griddle. (For best results, the heat should be medium to medium-low.) In a medium bowl or 1-quart measuring cup, combine flour and sugar. Set aside. In a 2-cup measuring cup, combine milk, egg, and oil; add to flour mixture, and stir until just blended. It's okay if the batter is lumpy. Pour about ¼ cup batter onto griddle. (If desired, lightly grease the griddle with butter.) Turn the pancakes over when bubbles form on top. Cook until second side is golden brown. Serve with your favorite syrup.

NOTE: *Self-rising flour is all-purpose flour with added salt and leavening (baking powder).*

# Gourmet Buttermilk Pancakes from Scratch

*Serves 2 or 3*

I used to resort to this classic recipe whenever I ran out of premade pancake mix. However, because of how light, fluffy, and tasty these always turn out, I don't even buy pancake mix anymore. The batter can be stored for a day or two in the refrigerator, and best of all, it's ultraeconomical. One batch costs less than a dollar!

*3 eggs, separated*

*3 tablespoons butter or margarine, melted*

*1⅔ cup buttermilk*

*1 teaspoon vanilla extract*

*1½ cups all-purpose flour*

*1 tablespoon sugar*

*1 teaspoon baking powder*

*1 teaspoon baking soda*

*½ teaspoon salt*

*Chopped pecans (optional)*

*Butter for greasing griddle (optional)*

Preheat a nonstick griddle. (For best results, the heat should be medium to medium-low.) In a large bowl, beat the egg yolks and butter. Add buttermilk and vanilla. Combine flour, sugar, baking powder, baking soda, and salt in another bowl; add to the egg mixture. Mix until just blended. (For thinner pancakes, add more buttermilk.) Beat egg whites until stiff peaks form; gently fold into batter. If desired, add a few tablespoons of chopped pecans. Pour about ¼ cup batter onto griddle. (If desired, lightly grease the griddle with butter.) Turn the pancakes over when bubbles form on top. Cook until second side is golden brown. Serve with your favorite syrup.

# Egg Salad Sandwich Filling

*Serves 2 to 4 (enough for 4 sandwiches)*

**6 hard-cooked eggs, peeled and chopped**
**1 medium stalk celery, chopped**
**⅓ cup mayonnaise**
**¼ teaspoon salt**
**¼ teaspoon pepper**
**Lettuce (optional)**

Mix all ingredients. Serve with lettuce, if desired, or on your favorite bread or crackers.

# Egg Flower Soup

*Serves 4*

*4 cups beef or chicken broth*

*2 eggs*

*1 teaspoon oil*

*2 stalks green onion, sliced*

*½ teaspoon salt*

Bring broth to a boil in a medium saucepan. Remove from heat. Beat the eggs and oil together in a small bowl. Pour into broth in a slow, steady stream, stirring slowly. Stir in green onions and salt.

# OTHER WAYS TO ENJOY EGGS

- **Make an egg sandwich** by placing your fried eggs on buttered toast and adding a slice of cheese, tomato, and pickle.
- **Huevos Rancheros** is a classic Mexican dish with fried eggs on corn tortillas, smothered with salsa and served with refried beans.
- **Egg Burritos** are a great "on the go" way to enjoy eggs. Fill warmed flour tortilla with scrambled eggs, roll up and enjoy.
- Get your veggies by creating an easy **Eggs Florentine.** Top cooked creamed spinach with fried eggs.
- **Poached eggs** are eggs cooked in boiling water. Heat 2 inches of water to boiling in a large skillet; reduce to a simmer. Break each egg into a measuring cup or a saucer. Holding the cup or saucer close to the water's surface, slip 1 egg at a time into the water. Cook for about 4 minutes and remove with slotted spoon. Serve on toast or English muffin.
- Make a **mock Eggs Benedict** by topping a toasted English muffin with a little butter, a slice of ham, and a fried or poached egg.

# 4.

# Can It, Sweetheart:
# The Virtues of Canned Food

You can fortify your diet with canned foods and feel very good about it. Canned fruits and vegetables are just as delicious and sometimes even more nutritious than their fresh or frozen counterparts, according to a study conducted in the fall of 1998 by the University of Illinois Department of Food Science. The study examined the nutritional content of thirty-five canned fruits, vegetables, legumes, fish, and poultry, and the nutritional value of five recipes made with canned, fresh, and frozen ingredients. Spaghetti sauce made with canned tomatoes provided more fiber, potassium, vitamins A and C, calcium, and iron as the same recipe prepared with fresh tomatoes. Canned red kidney beans ranked first in fiber content among the thirty-five products analyzed. The beans provide 9.2 grams of fiber per 1-cup serving. Canned salmon was found to contain more calcium than fresh or frozen products. (Canned fish in general is low in calories, high in omega-3 fatty acids and high in protein, B vitamins, potassium, and calcium.) A complete listing of the study results can be found at *www.aces.uiuc.edu/~nutrican*.

# FACTS ABOUT CANNED FOOD

- Canned food contains no preservatives. In fact, commercially-canned food is prepared essentially in the same way as home-canned food, using fresh ingredients that are cooked quickly at high temperatures and sealed in sterile containers.
- Canned fruits and vegetables are a good source of fiber, vitamins, and iron. Read the labels of canned foods to better appreciate their nutritional value.
- Most canned beans (black beans, red beans, butter beans, garbanzo beans, etc.) are nearly fat-free. They are high in fiber and may be used straight from the can to add flavor, color, and texture to a variety of meatless meals ranging from salads to casseroles.
- If you're looking for nondairy ways to increase your calcium intake, eat canned fish with the bones. You won't really notice the bones and you'll get as much calcium in a 3-ounce serving as you would from an 8-ounce glass of milk.
- Canned fruits and vegetables make it easy to meet your 5-a-Day goal for these foods.
- Steel cans are collected through more than 14,000 community recycling programs in the United States and Canada. When the collected cans are melted, the steel is recycled into an endless variety of new products, including cars, toys, bicycles, appliances, construction materials, and more food cans. To find out more about steel can recycling in your area, call the Steel Recycling Institute at 1-800-YES-I-CAN.

Always look for an "expiration date" or "best if used by date" on the can. If you cannot find a date on the can, then the general recommendation is to store canned food for no more than six months. For more information on food storage, see the Food Storage Index.

One last thing: always rinse or wipe the tops of the cans before opening to remove any dust that might have accumulated.

# Spicy Southwest Three-Bean Salad

*Serves 4 to 6*

*1 (15-ounce) can kidney beans, drained of all liquid*

*1 (15-ounce) can black beans, rinsed and drained of all liquid*

*1 (15-ounce) can green beans or yellow wax beans, drained of all liquid*

*1 cup bottled garlic vinaigrette salad dressing*

*2 tablespoons chili powder (less if you're not a fan of killer hot)*

Place the beans into a large bowl, pour the dressing, and sprinkle the chili powder over the mixture, tossing well to coat all. Serve at room temperature or cold.

# Ultimate Party Salad

*Serves 8*

This salad should be prepared in advance for best results. It's a great serve-yourself dish to bring to a potluck.

2 (14½-ounce) cans cut green beans, drained of all liquid

1 (14½-ounce) can wax beans, drained of all liquid

1 (4-ounce) can sliced black olives, drained of all liquid

1 (6-ounce) can button mushrooms, drained of all liquid

1 (6½-ounce) jar marinated artichoke hearts, including half the liquid

1 small red onion, thinly sliced

1 cup bottled Italian salad dressing

1 cup cherry tomatoes, sliced

½ cup Parmesan cheese (grated, shredded, or from the can)

Combine green beans, olives, mushrooms, artichoke hearts and liquid, onion, and dressing in large bowl. Cover and let marinate in refrigerator several hours or overnight. Just before serving, add sliced cherry tomatoes and Parmesan cheese. Mix thoroughly.

# Taco Salad

*Serves 4*

This salad packs in a lot of nutrition and takes only minutes to prepare.

 1 8-ounce bag ready-made salad
 1 medium tomato, chopped
 1 (15-ounce) can black beans, rinsed and drained of all liquid
 1 (11-ounce) can corn, drained of all liquid
 ½ cup (2 ounces) shredded cheddar cheese
 1 cup crushed tortilla chips
 Salad dressing, bottled or homemade

Combine all in a large salad bowl and serve with your favorite dressing. This salad goes well with cornbread.

# Very Easy Chili for Two

*Serves 2*

Most chili recipes are meant for a crowd and are never scaled down to serve just 1 or 2. You can always do the math and double or triple this recipe if you do have a crowd to feed.

*¼ pound ground beef*

*1 (15-ounce) can kidney beans, drained of all liquid*

*1 (14½-ounce) can diced tomatoes (see Note)*

*¼ teaspoon salt*

*1 teaspoon chili powder*

*2 tablespoons instant (or dried) minced onion*

In a nonstick skillet, brown meat, breaking up lumps with a wooden spoon. Add remaining ingredients, mixing well. Bring to a boil, reduce heat, cover and simmer for 20 minutes, stirring occasionally. Serve with crackers or cornbread.

NOTE: *Try the newer flavored canned diced tomatoes with added caramelized onions, jalapeños, and roasted garlic.*

# Can-Opener Chicken Casserole

*Serves 4 to 6*

1 (10½-ounce) can white chicken in broth or 1 (7-ounce) no-drain
   package chicken (located on shelf near the tuna)
1 (10½-ounce) can condensed cream of chicken soup
1 (10½-ounce) can chicken and rice soup
1 (12-ounce) can evaporated milk
1 (4-ounce) can mushrooms, drained of all liquid
1 (8½-ounce) can peas, drained of all liquid
1 (3-ounce) can chow mein noodles
1 (2.8-ounce) can fried onions
Slivered almonds (optional)

Preheat oven to 350°F. In a 3-quart casserole dish, stir together the first 7 ingredients. Bake, uncovered, for 30 minutes. Remove from oven and top with fried onions and slivered almonds, if desired. Return to oven for 15 minutes.

# Can-Opener Stew for a Crowd

*Serves 8 to 10*

This stew is not only hearty, it's also very handy because these ingredients are easy to keep in stock.

> 1 (24-ounce) can beef or chicken (you could also use canned beef stew
>     or a 17-ounce package of Hormel Beef Tips in Gravy,
>     found in the fresh meat aisle)
> 1 (14½-ounce) can diced tomatoes, undrained
> 1 (14¾-ounce) can creamed corn
> 1 (8½-ounce) can peas, drained of all liquid
> 1 (14½-ounce) can green beans, drained of all liquid
> 1 (14½-ounce) can carrots, drained of all liquid
> 1 (15-ounce) can sliced potatoes, drained of all liquid
> 1 tablespoon soy sauce
> 2 tablespoons Worcestershire sauce

Dump ingredients of all cans into very large soup pot. Add soy sauce and Worcestershire. Cook, stirring frequently, over medium heat until stew comes to a boil. Reduce heat to low, and simmer for 20 minutes. This stew goes great with cornbread.

### Microwave
Dump ingredients of all cans, plus soy sauce and Worcestershire, into a very large microwave-safe bowl. Stir. Heat on full power for 8 minutes.

# Tuna Casserole

*Serves 1 to 2*

Remember Mom's tuna noodle casserole? This is much easier and just as yummy!

*1 (6-ounce) can tuna or 3-ounce no-drain-can*
*1 (10½-ounce) can condensed cream of chicken soup*
*1 (5-ounce) can evaporated milk*
*1 (5-ounce) can chow mein noodles*
*1 teaspoon garlic salt*
*Shredded cheese of your choice (optional)*

Preheat oven to 350°F. Combine all ingredients except cheese in a 1- to 2-quart baking dish. Bake for 15 minutes or until heated through. If using cheese, sprinkle it on just after removing from oven.

### Microwave

Combine all ingredients except cheese in a 1- to 2-quart microwave-safe baking dish. Microwave on full power for 5 minutes. Sprinkle with cheese, if desired. Serve with sliced tomatoes.

# Hot Bean Dip

*Serves 1 or 2*

**1 (16-ounce) can refried beans**
**½ cup Pace Picante Sauce or any favorite salsa**
**Tortilla chips**

Combine ingredients in a medium saucepan over low heat, or place in a microwave-safe bowl and heat on full power for 1 minute. Serve with tortilla chips.

# Chili Con Queso Dip

*Serves 4 to 6*

1 (15-ounce) can mixed vegetables, drained of all liquid

1 (15-ounce) can chili with beans

1 medium tomato, chopped

1 cup (4 ounces) shredded cheddar cheese

⅛ teaspoon cumin

Tortilla chips

Preheat oven to 400°F. Combine ingredients in 2-quart baking dish. Bake uncovered for 15 minutes, until heated through and cheese is melted. Serve with tortilla chips or other chips.

# Oven-Roasted Garbanzos

*Serves 1 to 2*

This dish is great as a snack, tossed into a salad, or served over rice.

   1 (15½-ounce) can garbanzo beans (chickpeas),
      rinsed and drained of all liquid
   ¼ cup olive oil or 2 tablespoons sesame oil
   2 cloves garlic, finely minced
   Salt (optional)

Preheat oven 350°. Toss all ingredients together in a medium bowl and spread in a 13 × 9-inch baking pan or ovenproof casserole. Bake, stirring often, until golden browned, about 30 minutes. Sprinkle with salt, if desired.

# 5.

# Beyond Basic Ramen

Unless otherwise specified, use any ramen flavor you like. In most of the recipes, you are creating your own sauce or flavor enhancements, so I've suggested you discard the flavor packet or save it for another use.

At any given time you should be able to find ramen priced at ten for a dollar. You might also want to check out your local Asian market for different varieties of ramen. Many recipes call for crushed red pepper (keep leftover or unused packets of crushed red pepper from pizza parlors), but feel free to interchange your source of spiciness with anything that adds a good bite. Hot bean paste, hot chili paste, and pepper sauce would all work well.

# Buttery, Cheesy Ramen

*Serves 1*

**1 package ramen**

**2 tablespoons melted butter or margarine**

**¼ cup Parmesan cheese (grated, shredded, or from the can)**

Discard the ramen seasoning packet (or save it for another use). Prepare the ramen according to the package directions; drain and return to warm pan. Add the butter and cheese. Toss and serve warm. Tastes great with sliced tomatoes.

# Crispy Ramen Egg Foo Yong

*Serves 2*

The Puente boys' favorite after-school snack.

> *2 packages ramen*
> *2 eggs*
> *2 tablespoons soy sauce (see Note)*
> *2 tablespoons vegetable oil*

Prepare the ramen according to the package directions, reserving the flavor packets. When ramen is fully cooked, drain and set aside. Beat the eggs in a medium bowl, adding one flavor packet. (If you really want to you can add both, but I think it makes it too salty.) Add the soy sauce and drained noodles to the egg mixture. Heat the oil in a medium frying pan. When the oil is hot, add the noodle mixture. If you only have a small frying pan, cook the ramen in two batches. When the ramen is crispy on the bottom, flip over and cook until golden brown and crispy. Place on paper towel-lined plate to drain. Serve hot.

NOTE: *We love using Tabasco spicy soy sauce.*

# Pad Thai in a Hurry

*Serves 2*

This is one of my most requested dishes. Everyone loves it. It's even better the next day, after the flavors have blended.

SAUCE:

*2 tablespoons vegetable oil*

*¼ cup sugar*

*1 tablespoon white vinegar*

*1 tablespoon soy sauce*

*2 teaspoons crushed red pepper*

RAMEN:

*2 packages ramen*

*1 tablespoon peanut oil*

*2 cloves garlic, minced*

*¼ cup sesame seeds*

GARNISH (OPTIONAL)

*2 tablespoons chopped chives*

*2 tablespoons chopped peanuts*

Mix together the sauce ingredients in a small bowl and set aside. Prepare the ramen according to the package directions discarding the ramen seasoning packets (or saving them for another use). Drain the ramen and set aside in a covered dish to keep warm. Heat the peanut oil in a large skillet over medium heat. Add the garlic and sesame seeds and sauté for about 1 minute, or until the seeds are golden brown. Reduce the heat to medium-low; add the sauce mixture and heat for about 1 minute. Add ramen and toss until well-combined. Remove from heat. Sprinkle with the green onions and peanuts, if using, and serve immediately.

# Ramen and Beef

*Serves 2 to 3*

1 pound ground beef

1 package ramen

1 (11-ounce) can corn, drained of all liquid

1 (14½-ounce) can stewed tomatoes

    (try one of the snappier flavors for variety)

In a large skillet over medium heat, break up and cook the ground beef until browned. Drain off the fat. (Use any empty can, not the sink!) Sprinkle the flavor pack from the noodles over the beef and stir. Add the corn and stewed tomatoes. Bring to a boil. Break up the ramen noodles and add to the beef mixture. Reduce the heat to a simmer, cover, and cook for about 5 minutes.

*veggie*

# Ramen Florentine with Tofu

*Serves 1 or 2*

2 packages ramen

1 cup bottled Italian salad dressing

1 (10-ounce) package frozen chopped spinach,
   thawed

1 (6-ounce) package sliced fresh mushrooms

1 (14- or 16-ounce) cake firm tofu, drained,
   cut into bite-sized cubes

In a large saucepan, prepare the ramen according to package directions, adding the flavor packets. Drain off water and add dressing. Add spinach and mushrooms and stir around until the spinach has broken up and is well mixed with the ramen. Add tofu and stir. Serve warm.

NOTE: *You could use 10 ounces fresh spinach, chopped, if you happen to have it. You could also substitute one 6-ounce can of sliced mushrooms, drained of all liquid, instead of the fresh mushrooms.*

*veggie*

# Italian Ramen

*Serves 1*

1 package ramen

2 tablespoons olive oil

3 tablespoons Parmesan cheese (grated, shredded,
   or from the can), plus extra (optional)

2 cloves garlic, sliced

Your favorite herbs (oregano, basil,
   marjoram, or sage)

Discard the ramen seasoning packet (or save it for another use). Prepare the ramen according to the package directions. Drain the ramen and add the olive oil, Parmesan, garlic, and herbs. Stir well. Add additional Parmesan if desired. Serve with tossed green salad or sliced tomatoes.

# Ramen in Creamy-Spicy Peanut Sauce

*Serves 1*

1 package ramen

¼ cup creamy peanut butter

1 tablespoon hot water

1 tablespoon soy sauce

1 clove garlic, minced

1 tablespoon sugar

1 tablespoon rice vinegar

1 teaspoon sesame oil

1 teaspoon crushed red pepper, hot bean paste,
    or any favorite hot sauce

Discard the ramen seasoning packet (or save it for another use). In a medium saucepan, prepare the ramen according to package directions. To keep the noodles moist, drain off all but a tablespoon or two of the cooking liquid and return to warm pan. In a bowl, whisk together peanut butter, water, and soy sauce. Mix in garlic, sugar, vinegar, sesame oil, and red pepper. Toss with warm ramen.

# Creamy Ramen with Chicken

*Serves 2*

*1 cup broccoli florets*
*2 packages chicken-flavored ramen*
*1 (10½-ounce) can condensed cream of mushroom soup*
*½ soup can milk*
*1 cup cubed cooked chicken*

In a medium saucepan, bring 4 cups of water to a boil. Add the broccoli and the ramen. Cook for 3 to 4 minutes. Drain off all but a tablespoon or two of the cooking liquid. Stir in mushroom soup, milk, one of the seasoning packages, and the chicken. Heat through, stirring often. Serve hot.

# Ramen Salad

*Serves 2*

2 packages ramen
¼ cup olive or vegetable oil
1 tablespoon sugar
¼ cup almonds, toasted, slivered (see Note)
1 (10-ounce) package Broccoli Slaw Mix
    (found in fresh vegetable section of the market)

Crush the ramen noodles while still in the package. Open packages and pour noodles into a large bowl. Set aside. In another large bowl, mix one seasoning packet, oil, and sugar until sugar dissolves. Add almonds, and broccoli slaw. Add mixture to the dry noodles and toss until well-blended. Keep chilled until ready to serve.

NOTE: *Toast almonds on a cookie sheet in a 350°F oven for about 5 minutes or until they start to brown.*

*veggie*

# Warm Ramen Salad with Artichoke Hearts

*Serves 2*

*2 packages ramen*

*1 tablespoon lemon juice*

*1 clove garlic, minced*

*1 tablespoon of your favorite fresh herbs*
    *(oregano or parsley works best), chopped*

*1 (3-ounce) jar artichoke hearts in olive oil, undrained*

*Parmesan cheese (grated, shredded, or from the can)*

Discard the ramen seasoning packets (or save them for another use). Prepare the ramen according to the package directions; drain and return to warm pan. Add the lemon juice, garlic, herbs, and artichoke hearts with their liquid. Transfer to a serving bowl and sprinkle with Parmesan cheese. Serve warm.

# Sylvia's Foomie Salad

*Serves 4*

SALAD

1 small head green cabbage (about 1½ pounds),
   shredded

1 bunch green onions (scallions), chopped,
   both green and white parts

4 tablespoons toasted sesame seeds

½ cup slivered almonds, toasted (see Note)

2 packages uncooked ramen noodles, broken

DRESSING

¼ cup vegetable oil

1 tablespoon sesame oil

¼ cup rice vinegar

½ cup sugar

In a large serving bowl, mix all salad ingredients together. Chill. Mix all dressing ingredients together in a separate small bowl. Just before serving, pour dressing over salad and toss well.

NOTE: *Toast almonds on a cookie sheet in a 350°F oven for about 5 minutes or until they start to brown.*

# Tahini Ramen

*Serves 1*

1 package ramen

2 tablespoons tahini (sesame paste)

1 tablespoon soy sauce

2 cloves garlic, minced

1 teaspoon sugar

½ teaspoon crushed red pepper (optional)

Discard the ramen seasoning packet (or save it for another use). Prepare the ramen according to the package directions; drain and return to warm pan. Whisk together the tahini, soy sauce, garlic, sugar, and red pepper flakes, if using, in a small bowl until well combined. Pour over ramen and serve warm.

*veggie*

# Ramen with Vegetables

*Serves 3 to 4*

6 packages ramen noodles

1 small bunch broccoli florets

2 carrots, shredded

½ cup creamy peanut butter

3 tablespoons seasoned rice vinegar (rice vinegar
   with sugar added, found in the Asian food aisle)

3 tablespoons soy sauce

1 tablespoon sesame oil

2 teaspoons sugar

1 cup hot water

2 green onions, sliced thin

Discard the ramen seasoning packets (or save them for another use). In a large saucepan, prepare the ramen according to the package directions. After the ramen have cooked 4 minutes, add broccoli and carrots. Continue cooking 5 to 10 minutes, until the vegetables are tender but still crisp. Drain ramen mixture; return to saucepan.

Meanwhile, mix peanut butter, rice vinegar, soy sauce, sesame oil, sugar, and water with wire whisk or fork in a medium bowl until smooth. Add sauce to ramen mixture in saucepan, toss well. Spoon into large bowl; sprinkle with sliced green onions.

# Hot Curried Peanut Butter-Ramen Soup

*Serves 1*

1 package ramen

2 tablespoons chunky peanut butter

1 tablespoon crushed red pepper

   (use less if you're not a fan of super spicy)

2 cloves garlic, sliced

1 tablespoon curry powder

Prepare the ramen according to the package directions. (Using the flavor packet is optional and will make this dish salty.) Do not drain off the water. Over a low heat, add the peanut butter, crushed red pepper, garlic, and curry powder. Stir until everything is well blended. Cook for about 2 minutes more. Serve hot.

## IF YOU'RE REALLY IN A HURRY

There are ways to bump-up the ramen that take no time at all. I recommend discarding the ramen seasoning packet (but that's a personal preference, of course). Prepare the ramen according to the package directions, with or without the seasoning packet, drain and toss with any of the following ingredients:

- Szechwan sauce
- bottled Thai peanut sauce
- leftover meat, chicken, or even Spam
- canned chili beans
- garlic powder and chopped parsley
- garlic powder or garlic salt, and frozen peas or any frozen or canned vegetable
- nori (dried seaweed) and sesame seeds
- tofu
- hard-boiled eggs

# 6.

# Juicers and Blenders

This chapter is important for a few reasons. Many of you truly lack the time to prepare meals. Juicing and blender meals are much more than "quick fixes" to help prevent hypoglycemia or low blood sugar. (I'm sure you have experienced the symptoms: lightheadedness, blurred vision, needless fatigue and indecisiveness . . . okay, I'm a parent, just humor me on this one . . . all of which can interfere with performance.) Juicing is one of the very best ways to get your vitamins and minerals without a lot of fuss. In fact, juicing is the richest available food source of vitamins, minerals, and enzymes. It would be nearly impossible to eat enough raw fruits and vegetables in a day to nourish your body properly. For most people, four carrots, one apple, celery stalk, small beet, and a few handfuls of spinach would be too much for the body to take; they'd become bloated and gassy from all that fiber. But you could certainly drink the nutritional equivalent in a delicious, nutrient-rich glass of juice. I am absolutely convinced that the consumption of large amounts of fresh, organic fruit and vegetable juices saved my husband's health. And while the health issue was why we began to juice in the first place, it's now the fringe benefits that keep us juicing every day. My entire family has more energy than ever before. My day begins with a five-mile hike, and ends with helping my kids with their homework. And in between? Well, there are the final chapters for my next book, cooking for my family, and my frequent talk-show appearances. But increased energy is just the beginning. The teenagers in our family have clear, glowing skin, and you can too. You will never need to worry about overdosing on toxic amounts of vitamins, but you could actually and very easily exceed the recommended daily amounts for several key vitamins and minerals by as much as 500 percent. I urge you to learn more about the benefits of juicing by visiting a library or book store and reading some of the fabulous juicing books out there. I highly recommend anything by Jay "The Juiceman" Kordich, Michael T. Murray, or Stephen Blauer.

Unless otherwise noted, each of the following recipes serves one. The amounts listed are only a suggestion. If you want to add more of any ingredients, go ahead.

Refreshing smoothies can be anything you want them to be. Low-fat, nondairy, and vitamin-enriched, smoothies are sweet, nutritious, delicious, and easy to make. You can create an infinite variety of smoothies using your favorite fruits. If your favorite is out of season, use frozen fruit. For a tasty breakfast-on-the-go, a filling midafternoon snack, or just any time you're hungry and don't want to cook, my groovy smoothies are a treat.

I recommend freezing very ripe bananas to use in your smoothies. Peel bananas, discarding the skins. Arrange the bananas on a cookie sheet and place the sheet in the freezer for at least 30 minutes. The bananas should not touch one another, otherwise they will stick together. Once frozen, the bananas can be placed in an airtight bag or container without sticking together.

## The Puente Family's Favorite Breakfast

Oftentimes I will bring this drink right to the bed of one of my sleeping children. It's a million times better than waking up via an alarm clock.

*4 carrots*
*2 handfuls raw spinach*
*1 small beet, including the green tops*
*1 small apple, sliced and seeds removed*

Rinse all ingredients and push through the juicer.

# Glowing Skin

This one is packed with vitamins A, B, C, D, E, and K, as well as calcium, phosphorous, potassium, sodium, and trace minerals.

*4 carrots*
*1 small yam or sweet potato*
*1 small beet, including the green tops*

Rinse all ingredients and push through the juicer. You don't have to peel the yam, but do scrub it well.

# Spicy Vegetable Juice

If you're used to drinking vegetable juice from a can, you won't believe how fresh and different this tastes. It's fantastic for dieters because it's very low in calories, but very high in taste and nutrition. Leave out the Worcestershire and it's totally vegan.

1 carrot
1 fully ripe tomato
1 handful of raw spinach
1 celery stalk
1 small slice onion
1 clove garlic
2 radishes
Worcestershire
Tabasco

Rinse all the vegetables and push through the juicer. Start with only a few drops of Worcestershire and/or Tabasco and adjust to taste.

# Totally Cool

It is a well-known fact that celery and cucumbers will cool down the body during extreme heat. Serving this drink over ice will keep you refreshed even on a sweltering day. We take a large jug of it to summer sporting events.

*1 cucumber*
*2 celery stalks*
*1 apple or 1 cup grapes (or both)*

Rinse all ingredients and push through the juicer. You don't have to peel the cucumber.

# Immune Boost

This is a drink packed with antiviral and antioxidant effects. If colds are going around, drink this one for extra protection.

*1 orange, peeled*
*½ pineapple with skin, sliced*
*½ cup sliced strawberries*
*1 banana, peeled*

Juice the orange, pineapple, and strawberries; place in a blender with the banana and blend until smooth.

## Debbie's Lemonade

You won't believe how cool, refreshing, and delicious this is!

*3 apples, preferably a sweeter type over a tart kind*
    *(Fuji, red Delicious, Gala)*
*1 small lemon with peel*

Rinse the apples and lemon and push through juicer.

# BLENDER RECIPES AND MORE SMOOTHIES

*veggie*

## Banana Crunchy

1 cup soy, rice, or regular milk

1 banana, peeled and quartered

6 to 8 ice cubes

½ cup granola

Combine in blender. Pulse for 20 seconds or until smooth.

## Breakfast Bonanza

1 cup strawberry frozen yogurt or ice cream

1 banana, peeled and quartered

2 tablespoons frozen concentrated orange juice

1 tablespoon wheat germ

½ cup soy, rice, or regular milk

Combine in blender. Process until smooth and creamy.

# Banana Daiquiri

*1 cup orange juice*
*1 banana, peeled and quartered*
*Juice of 1 lime*

Combine in blender. Process until frothy.

# Fizzy Fruit

½ cup crushed pineapple, undrained

1 cup orange juice

1 small apple, peeled, cored, and diced

1 small pear, peeled, cored, and diced

1 cup sparkling water or club soda

Place all ingredients in a blender and blend until smooth.

# Cantaloupe Coolness

1 cup peeled, cubed cantaloupe

1 cup fresh or frozen unsweetened strawberries

1 cup green grapes

6 to 8 ice cubes

2 tablespoons sugar or more to taste

Place all ingredients in blender and process until smooth.

# High-Energy

1 cup vanilla yogurt or ice cream

1 cup peeled mango, or ½ cup sliced strawberries

1 tablespoon wheat germ

1 teaspoon honey, or more to taste

½ cup soy, rice, or regular milk

Place all ingredients in a blender. Blend at a low speed then gradually build to a high speed until smooth.

# Peanut Butter, Banana, and Jelly Milkshake

As good as the sandwich, and no crusts to cut off.

1 banana, peeled and quartered

1 tablespoon jelly, any flavor

1 tablespoon peanut butter

½ cup soy, rice, or regular milk

½ cup vanilla yogurt or ice cream

Place all ingredients in a blender and process until smooth and creamy.

# Chocolate-Banana Shake

½ cup soy, rice, or regular milk

1 banana, peeled and quartered

2 tablespoons chocolate syrup

½ teaspoon vanilla extract

1 cherry (optional)

Blend all ingredients until thick and frothy. Add a cherry on top and it's just like having a banana split!

# Date Shake

1 cup frozen vanilla yogurt *or* ice cream

½ cup soy, rice, *or* regular milk

3 tablespoons finely chopped dates

Blend all until creamy.

# Blueberry Yogurt Smoothie

½ cup (4 ounces) plain or vanilla yogurt

½ cup soy, rice, or regular milk

½ cup blueberries

6 to 8 ice cubes

Blend all ingredients until well combined.

NOTE: *Use any other fruit besides blueberries for this nutritious, delicious fruit smoothie . . . but be sure to remember to change the name!*

# Strawberry-Pineapple-Buttermilk Smoothie

*Enough for 2 if you care to share*

½ cup pineapple chunks, fresh or canned

1 cup strawberries, fresh or frozen

1 banana, peeled and quartered

2 cups buttermilk

2 tablespoons honey

4 ice cubes

Combine in blender until smooth.

# Tropical Smoothie

½ cup cream of coconut

1 banana, peeled and quartered

1 cup pineapple chunks, fresh or canned

If using canned pineapple, do not drain the liquid. Combine in blender until smooth.

# Kiwi-Banana Smoothie

2 kiwis, peeled and quartered

1 banana, peeled and quartered

½ cup orange juice

6 to 8 ice cubes

Blend all until smooth.

# High-Stamina Strawberry Shake

*1 cup sliced fresh or frozen strawberries*

*1 banana, peeled and sliced*

*½ cup vanilla yogurt*

*¼ cup soy, rice, or regular milk*

*2 tablespoons rice bran*

*1 tablespoon lemon juice*

*1 to 2 tablespoons honey*

Cover and freeze fresh strawberries and sliced bananas until firm, about 4 hours or overnight. If using frozen strawberries, do not thaw them. Combine strawberries, bananas, yogurt, milk, rice bran, lemon juice, and honey in blender. Process until smooth.

# Cinnamon Peach Smoothie

*Serves 2*

1 (15-ounce) can cinnamon-style peaches, or regular peaches
    with ½ teaspoon ground cinnamon
1 cup vanilla yogurt or ice cream
½ cup orange juice
1 banana, peeled and quartered
6 to 8 ice cubes

Combine ingredients in blender until smooth.

NOTE: *Canned peaches help to make this simple and available at any time. Try the other varieties of flavored peaches as well.*

# Creamy Cucumber Breakfast

This recipe is great on a warm summer morning.

> 1 small cucumber
> ½ cup buttermilk or plain yogurt
> 6 to 8 ice cubes

Peel cucumber; split in half lengthwise, and using a spoon, scoop out seeds. Place cucumber, buttermilk, and ice in blender. Process until very smooth.

# 7.

# Brown-Bagging It

You are on the run and your life is hectic. Eating at an unhurried and leisurely pace isn't a luxury you can afford. Brown-bagging it will save you time and money, and offers a big variety of choices.

To create the ultimate brown-bag lunch, one that will have your friends green with envy, you will need to plan accordingly, using this chapter as your guide. Here I will provide everything you'll need, including good tips to turn you into a brown-bag expert.

Use the pantry guide on page 12 for the basics. But for fun and variety, you may wish to have these items on hand too:

- bread: wheat, multigrain, potato, egg, rye, cinnamon–raisin, croissants, bagels, focaccia, and rolls of all kinds (remember, bread freezes well, so stock up if it's a good price)
- condiments and sauces that aren't so ordinary. Sweet-hot and Dijon mustards, horse-radish sauce, chili sauce, jalapeños, olives, capers, and pesto

- cheeses such as goat, jack, mozzarella, provolone, cheddar, Muenster, and Swiss
- trail mix or nuts and seeds
- sprouts, fresh spinach, and exotic greens such as arugula or romaine
- juice boxes (great for freezing and using as your ice pack)
- chips and crackers
- cream cheese in different flavors (found in bagel shops)
- assorted cold cuts
- cookies

## OTHER TIPS

- Save the small tubs and containers from margarine, yogurt, and other plastic cups with lids.
- Pack sandwiches in foil, zipper-lock plastic bags, or re-usable plastic sandwich containers.
- When packing vegetables and salads, separate them from the dressings and dips. This will keep the salads crisp and fresh-tasting.
- Pack crushable and delicate foods at the top of the lunch bag to avoid crushing.
- Pack the night before.
- Use frozen juice box drinks as an ice pack. Wrap the boxes in newspaper or a small bag to avoid the condensation that occurs when the juice thaws.
- And most importantly: keep your keys with your brown-bagged lunch so you won't forget to take it with you!

# Joey's Ranch Dressing in a Pinch

Use this as a sandwich spread, salad dressing, or dip.

*½ cup mayonnaise*
*3 tablespoons juice from an olive or a pickle jar*
    *(usually a mixture of vinegar, garlic,*
    *herbs, and spices)*

Mix the mayonnaise and olive or pickle juice together, adjusting the amounts to suit your taste. Store unused dressing in the refrigerator.

# Joey's Spicy Dip

Use this as a sandwich spread, salad dressing, or dip.

*½ cup mayonnaise or ranch dressing*

*3 tablespoons hot chili sauce*

Mix the mayonnaise and hot chili sauce together, adjusting the amounts to suit your taste. Store unused sauce in the refrigerator.

## THE FILLING

The following recipes are for sandwich fillings. Be as creative as you wish by choosing different breads and condiments.

## Boiled Chicken for Chicken Sandwiches

Refrigerate what you will use within 2 days and freeze the remainder in zipper-lock plastic bags.

> *1 pound chicken parts, any kind*
> *1 teaspoon salt*
> *2 cups chicken broth or (if you're over 21) ½ cup white wine*
>    *mixed with 1½ cups water*
> *1 tablespoon black ground pepper*

Place the chicken in a large pot and sprinkle with salt. Add the chicken broth and pepper. Place the pot over a medium-high heat and bring to a boil. Reduce the heat to low, cover the pot and simmer for 20 minutes, until the chicken is no longer pink. Remove the chicken from the pot, discard the liquid, cool the chicken, remove the skin and bones, and proceed with any of the following recipes.

# Curried Chicken Salad

*Yields enough for 4 large sandwiches*

I recommend serving this on croissants or egg bread, or stuffed into pita pockets. If desired, add some fresh lettuce too.

*½ cup mayonnaise*

*1 teaspoon lemon juice*

*2 tablespoons curry powder*

*2 cups cooked chicken, chopped*

*½ cup celery, chopped*

*½ cup seedless grapes, halved, or raisins*

*¼ cup chopped almonds or walnuts*

Blend mayonnaise, lemon juice, and curry powder in a small bowl. Set aside. Combine chicken, celery, grapes, and almonds in a large bowl. Mix mayonnaise mixture into chicken. Chill at least 1 hour before serving.

# Southwestern Chicken

*Yields enough for 2 large burritos or tostadas*

Serve this on crispy tostada shells, or roll in large flour tortillas.

1 cup cooked chicken, chopped

½ small red onion, chopped or diced very small

1 tomato (preferably a plum tomato), chopped or diced very small

¼ cup fresh cilantro, minced

Juice from ½ lime

½ teaspoon ground cumin

Chili or pepper sauce

Blend all in a large mixing bowl. Chill for at least an hour to blend the flavors.

## MORE IDEAS FOR VERY SIMPLE SANDWICHES USING COOKED OR CANNED CHICKEN

Chicken, lettuce, sliced tomatoes, and mayonnaise on white or whole-wheat bread

Chicken, bacon, lettuce, and cheddar cheese on potato bread

Chicken, sliced onion, and fresh spinach on white bread

Chicken, cucumbers, and hummus in pita bread

Chicken, avocado, sprouts, and honey mustard on multigrain bread

Chicken, grilled onions, and barbecue sauce on a sesame seed roll

## PEANUT BUTTER SANDWICHES AND RELATED RECIPES

Peanut butter was first developed in 1890. Natural peanut butter is a blend of ground shelled peanuts, oil, and a small amount of salt. Most peanut butter can be stored at room temperature for up to 6 months. Peanut butter is an excellent way to get protein into your diet.

You all are familiar with the basic peanut butter and jelly on white bread, of course. Now treat yourself to a "fancier" peanut butter sandwich with these ideas. (Also see the index for other recipes that include peanut butter.)

Peanut butter and honey with toasted sesame seeds on egg bread

Peanut butter and tofu with tomato and alfalfa sprouts on wholegrain bread

Peanut butter and sliced banana on waffles

Peanut butter and marshmallow fluff on white bread

Peanut butter and bacon on sourdough toast

Peanut butter and sliced bananas with honey on egg bread

Peanut butter stuffed into celery, sprinkled with raisins

Peanut butter with sliced apples or apple butter on a bagel

Peanut butter and granola (or any favorite cereal) on sourdough bread

Peanut butter and crushed potato chips on white bread

Peanut butter and cream cheese, with or without jam on bagel

# Basic Tuna Salad

*Yields enough for 2 sandwiches*

Like chicken salad, tuna salad is deliciously simple and very basic. Among the extras you can add to the basic recipe are chopped cashews, peanuts, or walnuts; cubes of cheese; slices of cucumber; diced green or red bell peppers; capers; hot sauce; and minced garlic. Serve on any favorite bread.

*1 (6-ounce) can of water-packed tuna, drained*
*½ cup diced celery*
*¼ cup mayonnaise*
*2 tablespoons finely chopped red onion*
*Salt and pepper*

Dump the tuna into a large mixing bowl and flake with a fork. Combine the tuna with the celery, mayonnaise, and onion. Add salt and pepper a little at a time, taste, and adjust to your liking.

# Tuna Melt

*Yields enough for 4 open-face sandwiches*

Feel free to substitute cheddar or any other cheese for the Monterey Jack.

*Basic Tuna Salad, page 99*
*4 slices bread, toasted*
*4 ounces Monterey Jack cheese, grated*

Preheat the broiler. Prepare Basic Tuna Salad. Divide the tuna salad among 4 slices of toast and top with grated Monterey Jack cheese. Broil the sandwiches on a baking pan about 5 inches from the heat until the cheese is melted and bubbling, 1 to 2 minutes. Serve hot.

# BLT

*Serves 2*

One of America's favorite sandwiches, the BLT can be dressed up by adding avocado slices, bean sprouts, and cheddar cheese. You can microwave or pan-fry the bacon.

6 slices bacon
4 slices bread, toasted
2 tablespoons mayonnaise
1 beefsteak or other meaty tomato,
    sliced about ¼-inch thick
4 leaves lettuce

To microwave bacon, place 3 or 4 paper towels on a microwave-safe plate. Place bacon on top of paper towels. Cook at full power 1 minute for each slice of bacon. To pan-fry bacon, place bacon in a cold frying pan in a single layer. Cook over medium heat until bacon begins to crisp. Turn each piece over and cook on the other side until desired crispness. Drain on paper towels.

Lay out your toast on a work surface or cutting board. Spread the mayonnaise evenly on each slice of toast. Divide the tomato, lettuce, and bacon among two slices of toast, and top with the remaining toast, pressing together.

# Avocado and Sprouts Sandwich

*Serves 1*

A California classic!

    *2 slices whole-wheat bread*
    *1 tablespoon mayonnaise*
    *2 slices Swiss or provolone cheese*
    *1 thick slice ripe tomato*
    *1 small ripe avocado, peeled and cut into slices*
    *Sunflower or bean sprouts*

Spread the bread with mayonnaise. Layer cheese, tomato, avocado, and sprouts on one side, slap together, and enjoy.

# Sloppy Toms

*Serves 1*

This tomato sandwich is messy but very tasty.

*1 ripe tomato, preferably homegrown*
*Butter, softened*
*2 slices bread, toasted*
*Mayonnaise*
*¼ teaspoon salt*
*Pinch of sugar*
*Pepper*

Slice the tomato into three thick slices. Butter both slices of toast, then spread a thick layer of mayonnaise on both pieces. Place the tomato slices on one slice of the toast and season with the salt, sugar, and black pepper. Put it all together, and using lots of napkins, enjoy!

# Make Your Own Trail Mix

*Yields enough for 10 servings*

1 cup unsalted raw or roasted peanuts, cashews, or almonds

1 cup sunflower seeds

1 cup coconut chips

1 cup chocolate chips

1 cup raisins

Mix all ingredients together. Keep it fresh by storing in airtight containers.

# 8.

# Hot from the Oven
# (Yes, you have to wear those little mitts!)

Oven baking requires an ovenproof casserole or baking dish, 1- to 3-quart size, which comes in ceramic, glass, clay, stainless steel, or other metals. (A 1-quart casserole holds 4 cups. If you're uncertain about the capacity of a baking dish, use a measuring cup to check.) It's important to choose the proper size casserole dish for your recipe. If it's too large, you will end up with a dried-out casserole. If it's too small, you run the risk of your food bubbling up and spilling over.

In the recipes that call for chicken pieces, I usually advise rinsing the chicken pieces before using. Because there's the danger of salmonella poisoning, always wash your hands after handling raw chicken.

## BAKED POTATOES AND VARIATIONS

Potatoes come in different varieties. The best potato to use for baking is the Idaho, also known as russet. Its low moisture and high starch content not only give it superb baking qualities but also make it excellent for french fries. Rubbing the outside of the potatoes with vegetable oil before baking will help them absorb more heat and cook faster. It also makes the skins crisp and nicely brown. For soft skins, wrap each potato in foil before baking.

## Basic Baked Potatoes

Make four at a time, wrapping and refrigerating the leftovers for up to three days. Reheat in the microwave, 3 minutes on full power for each potato.

Preheat oven to 425°F. Scrub potatoes with a brush. Prick potatoes with a fork. Wrap each in foil and bake for 40 to 60 minutes. Using hot pads, remove from the oven, and keep in foil until ready to serve. Just before serving cut a crisscross in the top. Press ends and push up. Serve the traditional way with butter, sour cream, and chives or try one of the following toppings:

- **Texas Taters:** Chili beans and shredded cheddar cheese
- **German Spuds:** Sauerkraut, diced smoked sausage, and Thousand Island dressing
- **Gourmet Potatoes:** Sautéed mushrooms, cream cheese, and diced shallots or chopped chives
- **Garden Potatoes:** Chopped broccoli, dried or chopped fresh parsley, and ranch dressing
- **Parmesan Potatoes:** Mayonnaise and Parmesan cheese mixed together with a dash of pepper, spooned on top of potato. (This is one of our personal favorites!)
- **Southwest Potatoes:** Black beans, salsa, sour cream, and chopped cilantro
- **Low Fat Potatoes:** Equal amounts low-fat unflavored yogurt and low-fat cottage cheese

- **Ranch Potatoes:** Creamy ranch dressing and diced red or yellow bell peppers
- **Hearty Potatoes:** Baked beans and crumbled bacon
- **For Southerners Only:** Black-eyed peas and creamy gravy
- **For Californians Only:** Avocado slices and sprouts
- **Decadent, Throw-the-Diet-out-the-Window Potatoes:** Softened butter, grated cheddar cheese, sour cream, chopped green onion tops or chives, and a dash of salt

*veggie*

# Garlic-Roasted Rosemary Potatoes

*Serves 2*

12 (about 1½ pounds) new red or other all-purpose potatoes,
   quartered (see Note)
½ cup olive oil
4 large cloves garlic, minced
2 tablespoons chopped fresh rosemary or 1 tablespoon dried
Salt and pepper

Preheat oven to 400°F. Coat potatoes with olive oil, garlic, fresh rosemary, and salt and pepper. Spread in one layer in a shallow baking dish. Bake for one hour or until crisp.

Variation
Parboil the potatoes in advance. Follow above directions, reducing the roasting time to 15 minutes.

NOTE: *All-purpose potatoes are more moist than baking potatoes and will hold together in boiling water. They are better than russets for using in soups and stews and are great for mashed potatoes.*

# Potato and Cheese Puff

*Serves 4*

6 medium red, Yukon Gold, or other all-purpose potatoes,
    peeled and cubed (see Note, page 108)
1 cup (4 ounces) shredded cheddar cheese,
    plus extra for garnish
¾ cup milk
2 tablespoons butter or margarine at room temperature,
    plus extra for greasing the baking dish
1 teaspoon salt
1 egg, beaten

Preheat oven to 350°F. Place the potatoes in a saucepan and cover with water. Over a medium-high heat, bring to a boil. Cook until tender, about 15 minutes. Drain and mash; return to warm pan. Add the cheese, milk, butter, and salt; cook and stir over low heat until cheese and butter are melted. Fold in egg. Spread into a greased baking dish. Bake, uncovered, for 20 to 25 minutes. Sprinkle with extra cheese, and bake 5 minutes longer or until golden brown.

# Broccoli and Cheese Puff

*Serves 4*

1½ *cups Bisquick or other biscuit mix*

1½ *cups milk*

2 *cups (8 ounces) shredded cheddar and jack cheese mix*

1 *(10-ounce) package frozen chopped broccoli, thawed*

**Butter for greasing casserole**

Preheat oven to 350°F. Mix all ingredients in a large bowl and pour into a buttered casserole. Bake for 45 minutes. Serve hot. Delicious with fresh fruit.

# Corn Soufflé

*Serves 4*

3 eggs
1 cup (4 ounces) shredded cheddar cheese
1 can (14¾ ounce) creamed corn
¾ cup Bisquick or other biscuit mix
1 (4 ounce) can chopped green chiles
**Butter for greasing casserole**

Preheat oven to 350°F. Mix all ingredients well in a large bowl and pour into a buttered casserole. Bake for 40 minutes. Serve hot. This dish goes well as a side dish to a Mexican entrée.

# Chile Relleno Casserole

*Serves 4*

1 (14-ounce) can whole green chiles, drained of all liquid

Butter for greasing casserole

2 cups (8 ounces) grated cheddar and jack cheese mix

3 eggs, beaten

1 (12-ounce) can evaporated milk

½ teaspoon salt

½ teaspoon pepper

2 tablespoons all-purpose flour

Preheat oven to 350°F. Layer chiles in a greased baking dish. Top with cheese. In a medium bowl, combine eggs, milk, salt, pepper, and flour. Pour over cheese and chiles. Bake for 45 minutes or until bubbly and golden brown on top. Serve with rice and beans or simply alongside a tossed green salad.

# Hot Cheese Bread

*Serves 2*

1 small French bread loaf (about 8 ounces),
  sliced in half lengthwise
½ cup mayonnaise
1 cup (about 4 ounces) grated cheese of your choice
  (Parmesan or jack work great)
1 (4-ounce) can diced green chiles, drained (optional)

Preheat oven to 350°F. Place bread, cut side up, on a cookie sheet. Combine mayonnaise and cheese (and green chiles if using) and spread over bread. Bake for 10 minutes. Serve warm.

# Candied Bacon for a Party

*Serves 6*

As simple as this sounds, it is always the biggest hit at a party or potluck get-together. It's a classic recipe from my first book, *Deceptively Simple*.

*1 pound sliced bacon*

*1 cup sweet-and-hot mustard*

*¼ cup brown sugar*

Preheat oven to 400°F. Measure out ½ cup of the mustard, reserving the extra to use as dip. Brush each slice of bacon with mustard and sprinkle with brown sugar. Roll up and place seam side down on a jelly roll pan or a large baking dish. (Don't use a flat cookie sheet because the fat from the bacon will spill.) Cook about 15 minutes. Remove from baking dish and arrange on a platter with the reserved dip. Serve hot.

# Cheesy Chicken Enchiladas

*Serves 2*

Do you have leftover chicken? If so, use it in this delicious dish.

*1 cup salsa*
*2 cups chopped or shredded cooked chicken*
*2 cups (8 ounces) shredded cheddar or jack cheese*
*4 large flour tortillas*

Preheat oven to 350°F. Place ½ cup of the salsa, all of the chicken, and 1 cup of the cheese in a saucepan or microwave-safe container. Heat just until warmed, about 5 minutes over the stove, or 1 minute on full power in the microwave. Spread remaining salsa in a small baking dish. Divide warm chicken mixture in center of each tortilla; roll up. Place tortillas, seam-side down, on salsa. Top with remaining cheese. Bake for 20 minutes. Serve with tossed green salad.

# Pork Chops and Corn

*Serves 2*

*Butter or vegetable-oil spray for greasing casserole*

*4 pork chops (1 to 1½ pounds, with or without bones)*

*1 teaspoon salt, adjust to taste*

*1 teaspoon pepper, adjust to taste*

*2 (15-ounce) cans cream-style corn*

Preheat oven to 350°F. Place pork chops in a greased 2-quart baking dish. Season with salt and pepper. Pour corn over pork chops. Bake for 30 minutes.

# Classic Roast Whole Chicken

*Serves 4*

Whole chickens are the least expensive way to buy chicken. The average whole chicken weighs 2 to 4 pounds. Serve this dinner with baked potatoes and fresh vegetables and you have a feast for your whole dorm or for all your friends for less than the cost of one super-sized fast food meal. Check your local paper's food section for specials.

> *1 whole chicken (3 to 4 pounds) rinsed with cold water*
>    *and dried with paper towels*
> *1 tablespoon butter, softened*
> *1 teaspoon dried thyme or sage (or a mixture of both)*

Preheat oven to 475°F. Place chicken breast-down on rack in roasting pan. Rub butter over chicken. Sprinkle thyme over chicken. Add enough water to cover bottom of pan. Roast for 10 minutes. Reduce oven temperature to 375°F. Carefully turn chicken breast-side up. Roast for 90 minutes or until chicken is browned. To be sure the chicken is cooked through, puncture with a long-handled fork near one of the legs. The juices should be clear, not pink. Remove from oven and let stand about 5 minutes before cutting and serving.

Use the leftovers (if there are any leftovers) for Cheesy Chicken Enchiladas on page 115.

# Baked Barbecued Chicken

*Serves 4*

*8 chicken pieces (about 2 pounds), with or without skin*
*1 cup of your favorite bottled barbecue sauce*

Preheat oven to 350°F. Rinse chicken with cold water and pat dry with paper towels. Arrange chicken skin-side up in one layer in a large baking pan. Pour barbecue sauce over chicken. Bake uncovered for 45 minutes or until chicken is tender and cooked through. Serve hot. This dish goes well with the Hot Cheese Bread on page 113 and a tossed green salad.

# Easy Chicken Bake

*Serves 4*

8 chicken pieces (about 2 pounds), with or without skin
1 tablespoon melted butter
1 (10½-ounce) can condensed cream of chicken soup

Preheat oven to 375°F. Rinse chicken with cold water and pat dry with paper towels. Place chicken skin-side up in one layer in a baking dish. Drizzle with melted butter. Bake 30 minutes. Spoon soup over chicken. Bake 30 minutes more or until chicken is no longer pink. Remove chicken from oven and stir sauce, incorporating the soup with the chicken drippings. Serve over rice (pages 133–134 or 139) or potatoes (see Index for potato recipes).

# Sesame Chicken

*Serves 2 to 4*

**4 to 6 chicken pieces (thighs work best)**
**3 tablespoons honey**
**¼ cup sesame seeds**
**Salt and pepper (optional)**

Preheat oven to 350°F. Rinse chicken with cold water and pat dry with paper towels. Place chicken skin-side up in one layer in a baking pan, preferably with a nonstick coating. Drizzle honey over chicken and sprinkle the sesame seeds over each piece. Bake for 35 to 45 minutes, or until the chicken is tender and no longer pink. Season with salt and pepper if desired. Serve over any favorite rice.

# Asian-Style Mini-Drumsticks

*Serves 2*

*12 to 16 mini-drumsticks, also known as drumettes*
   *(from the upper wing of the chicken)*
   *or 6 to 8 regular drumsticks*
*½ cup brown sugar, packed lightly into measuring cup*
*½ cup soy sauce*
*⅛ teaspoon ground ginger*
*2 tablespoons toasted sesame seeds (optional)*

Rinse chicken with cold water and pat dry with paper towels. Place chicken in one layer in a baking pan, preferably with a nonstick coating. Combine the sugar, soy sauce, ginger, and sesame seeds (if using) in a small bowl, mixing well. Pour mixture over chicken and marinate in the refrigerator, covered, at least 30 minutes. While chicken is marinating, heat oven to 350°F. Bake chicken for 25 to 35 minutes if using mini drumsticks, 45 minutes if using regular. Great served over rice (see pages 133–134 and 149).

# Paper-Wrapped Chicken

*Serves 4*

This is a fun dish to take to a potluck party. It's very easy and everyone likes it. Best of all, it's a simple clean up. This should actually be called "foil-wrapped chicken" because you will need foil wrap to make this. For best results, allow plenty of time (up to 24 hours) for the chicken to soak in the marinade.

*1 pound skinless and boneless chicken breasts,*
  *cut into 1 × 1-inch pieces*
*2 green onions, trimmed and chopped*

MARINADE:
*1 tablespoon soy sauce*
*1 tablespoon hoisin or teriyaki sauce*
*1 tablespoon vegetable oil*
*1 teaspoon sesame oil*
*1 clove garlic, minced*
*¼ teaspoon pepper*
*1 teaspoon sugar*
*2 teaspoons cornstarch*

Place chicken in a shallow pan. Sprinkle green onions on top of chicken. In a small bowl, mix the soy sauce, hoisin, vegetable and sesame oils, garlic, pepper, sugar, and cornstarch together; pour mixture over chicken. Cover pan with wax paper or plastic wrap and place in refrigerator. Marinate chicken for at least 2 hours, or as much as 24 hours.

Preheat oven to 450°F. Wrap 2 or 3 chicken pieces in foil and place in a single layer on a cookie sheet. Bake for 12 minutes. Serve hot.

# Oven-Fried Chicken

*Serves 2 to 4*

Whip up a batch the night before a picnic. It's good cold too.

> *4 to 6 chicken pieces (drumsticks work great)*
>   *(about 1½ pounds)*
> *1 cup bread crumbs*
> *1 teaspoon salt*
> *1 teaspoon pepper*
> *¼ cup mayonnaise*

Preheat oven to 350°F. Rinse chicken with cold water and pat dry with paper towels. Place the bread crumbs in a shallow plate and add the salt and pepper, mixing well. Spread some of the mayonnaise on each piece of chicken and dip in crumbs to coat heavily. Place on a cookie sheet or in an ovenproof baking dish and bake for 45 minutes or until the chicken is no longer pink. If you're using larger pieces of chicken, bake for 1 hour.

# Jill's Corn Flake Crumb-Baked Chicken

*Serves 2 to 4*

This is so crisp and delicious, yet it only takes minutes to prepare.

**4 to 6 chicken pieces (about 1½ pounds)**
**1 cup regular or fat-free bottled Italian salad dressing**
**1 cup corn flake crumbs (see Note)**

Preheat oven to 350° to 375°F. Rinse chicken with cold water and pat dry with paper towels. Dip each piece into Italian dressing, then into the corn flake crumbs, coating thoroughly. Place onto a rack in a roasting pan and bake 1 to 1¼ hours. Test for doneness by cutting into largest piece. Juices should run clear.

NOTE: *Corn flake crumbs are available in the grocery store—usually found in the bread crumbs section—or make your own by finely crushing corn flakes.*

# Baked Chicken Reuben

*Serves 2 to 4*

**4 to 6 chicken pieces (about 1½ pounds)**
**Butter for greasing casserole**
**1 (14½-ounce) can sauerkraut, drained of all liquid**
**4 slices (about 4 ounces) Swiss cheese**
**1¼ cup bottled Thousand Island salad dressing**
**Rye bread (optional)**

Preheat oven to 325°F. Rinse chicken with cold water and pat dry with paper towels. Arrange chicken in lightly greased casserole. Place sauerkraut over chicken. Top with Swiss cheese. Pour dressing evenly over cheese. Cover with foil and bake for 1½ hours. Serve with rye bread, if desired.

# Baked Chicken and Stuffing

*Serves 2 to 4*

4 chicken breast halves, about 1¼ pound (see Note)

Butter for greasing casserole

1 (10½ ounce) can condensed cream of chicken
  or cream of mushroom soup

¼ cup chicken broth, or if you're over 21, dry white wine

1 (6-ounce) box stuffing mix, crushed

¼ cup (½ stick) butter, melted

Preheat oven to 350°F. Rinse chicken with cold water and pat dry with paper towels. Arrange chicken in lightly greased casserole. In a small bowl, combine soup and chicken broth or wine and spoon over chicken; sprinkle with stuffing mix. Drizzle butter over top. Cover loosely with foil. Bake for 45 to 55 minutes, or until chicken is no longer pink. Just before serving, toss the stuffing with the sauce to moisten. Serve with mashed potatoes and peas.

NOTE: *Skinless, boneless chicken breasts work the best in this recipe. If you scan the food section of your local paper you can usually find specials as low as $2.00 per pound.*

# Honey-Mustard Chicken

*Serves 2 to 4*

For best results, start marinating the chicken the day before.

*4 to 6 chicken pieces (about 1½ pounds)*
*½ cup honey*
*½ cup Dijon mustard*
*1 tablespoon curry powder*
*2 tablespoons soy sauce*

Rinse chicken with cold water and pat dry with paper towels. Place chicken in a baking dish. Mix together honey, mustard, curry, and soy sauce. Pour over chicken and marinate at least 1 hour. While chicken is marinating, preheat oven to 350°F. Bake, covered with foil, for 1 hour. Remove foil, baste chicken with pan juices and cook, uncovered, an additional 15 minutes. Serve with white rice and broccoli.

# Roast Turkey

*Serves a crowd*

*1 turkey, any size (nothing will go to waste if you use*
  *the leftovers for sandwiches, salads, and soups)*
*2 tablespoons melted butter or vegetable oil*
*1 tablespoon salt*
*1 tablespoon pepper*
*1 tablespoon paprika or poultry seasoning*
*Garlic and herbs (optional)*
*Vegetable oil (optional)*

If your turkey is frozen, allow it 2 or 3 days to thaw in the refrigerator. Remove the packet of innards and gizzards from the cavity. Cook it up for the cat if you wish. Rinse turkey in cold water and pat dry with paper towels. Transfer to a large bowl. With your hands, coat the turkey with the melted butter and sprinkle the salt, pepper, and paprika all over. If desired, for more flavor, stuff the cavity with peeled garlic cloves (as many as you want) and fresh herbs (rosemary, sage, whatever you happen to like).

Preheat the oven to 325°F. Place the turkey in a large roasting pan and add 1 or 2 cups of water. It's a good idea to tie the turkey's legs together with kitchen string (not plastic), but don't panic if you don't have any. Just try to tuck the legs in so they're not sticking out all over the place. Put the turkey in the oven. It's important to baste the turkey often (every 30 minutes or so) while cooking. Basting with vegetable oil and/or the turkey's juices helps to keep the bird moist and juicy.

How to tell when the turkey is done: If you have a meat thermometer, it will register at 170°F. If you poke the turkey in the thigh with a fork, the juices will run clear. An average turkey weighing about 14 pounds will take about 3½ hours.

NOTE: *Don't throw the turkey carcass out. Make turkey soup. See recipe page 146.*

# Tex-Mex Casserole

*Serves 4*

1 pound ground beef
3 cups crushed corn chips
Butter for greasing casserole
1 (19-ounce) can enchilada sauce
2 cups (about 8 ounces) shredded jack cheese
Sour cream

Preheat oven to 350°F. In skillet, brown ground beef. Drain excess fat; discard fat and set aside meat. Place 2 cups of the corn chips in bottom of a greased medium ovenproof casserole. Pour ground beef over chips. Pour enchilada sauce over ground beef. Top with cheese. Bake 25 minutes or until bubbly and hot. Sprinkle remaining corn chips over top of casserole. Bake an additional 5 minutes. Serve with a dollop of sour cream.

### Microwave

Crumble ground beef in medium microwave-safe baking dish. Cover and microwave on full power for 3 minutes. Stir to break up ground beef. Recover and microwave on full power for 3 minutes or until thoroughly cooked. Drain excess fat; discard set aside meat. Place 2 cups of the corn chips in bottom of a greased medium microwave-safe casserole. Pour ground beef over chips. Pour enchilada sauce over ground beef. Top with cheese. Cook at full power for 7 minutes or until bubbly and hot. Sprinkle remaining corn chips over top of casserole. Serve with a dollop of sour cream.

# Simple Baked Fish

*1 pound cod or other white fish fillets*
*Butter for greasing baking dish*
*1 tablespoon olive oil*
*½ teaspoon salt*
*¼ teaspoon lemon-pepper*

Preheat oven to 375°F. Arrange fillets in 1 layer in a greased baking dish. Drizzle with oil and season with salt and lemon-pepper. Bake about 12 minutes or until fish is opaque (non-transparent) throughout. Serve with Glazed Carrots, page 162.

# Hash Brown Potato Casserole

*Serves 4 to 6*

*1 (28-ounce) bag frozen hash brown potatoes, thawed*

*½ cup (1 stick) butter, plus extra for greasing baking dish*

*1 (10½-ounce) can condensed cream of mushroom*
*    or cream of celery soup*

*2 cups sour cream*

*¾ cup milk*

*1 cup (4 ounces) grated cheddar cheese*

Preheat oven to 350°F. Spread thawed potatoes into a well-greased 9 × 13-inch baking dish. In large saucepan over medium heat, combine butter and soup until butter is melted. Remove from heat and stir in sour cream and milk until well-blended. Pour soup mixture over potatoes. Top with cheese. Bake for 45 minutes. Eat as a main dish or as a hearty side to a chicken entrée.

# 9.

# Skillet and Other
# Stovetop Skills

S killets, also known as frying or sauté pans, are low pans with tapered or straight sides and
one handle sticking out. If you can only have one skillet, it's a good idea to have a tight-
fitting lid to go with it. You also want your pan to be heavy-bottomed for even cooking.
A ten-inch diameter is the ideal size for most recipes.

Covered saucepans are a must in your kitchen. Two-, four-, and six-quart sizes are the most
popular for most recipes. As with skillets, look for heavy bottoms and tight-fitting lids.


## RICE

There are recipes that incorporate rice throughout this book. See the index for a complete listing.

At about 4 cents per serving, nothing beats the value and versatility of rice. Of course you can
always cook rice according to package instructions, and you will end up with good rice. However,

why not end up with great rice? It's easy when you replace the cooking water with chicken or vegetable broth; fun and tasty when you add interesting and varied foods items such as:

- **Maui Rice:** Crushed pineapple and green bell pepper slices
- **Veggie Variety:** Steamed zucchini, carrots, or broccoli, and butter
- **Easy Cheesy:** Butter and Parmesan cheese
- **Saint Patrick's Rice:** Peas and chopped parsley
- **BLT Rice:** Crumbled bacon, shredded lettuce, chopped tomato, and sour cream
- **Quick and Sweet:** Cinnamon, sugar, and butter OR vanilla ice cream and cinnamon
- **Scrumptious Sesame:** Toasted sesame seeds, sesame oil, and chopped green onions
- **Fitness Rice:** Toasted sunflower seeds, raisins, and dried fruit
- **Gourmet Rice:** Mushrooms, snow peas, and garlic cooked in butter, with minced shallots
- **Only-If-You-Don't-Have-a-Date Rice:** Onions and garlic cooked in butter
- **It's Greek to Me:** Feta cheese and olives
- **Curry-in-a-Hurry:** Curry powder, raisins, and chopped nuts

## RICE GUIDE

Not all rice is the same. You may wish to experiment with the different types of rice to see what you like best.

**Long-grain white rice:** all-purpose rice; cooks up white and fluffy

**Short-grain white rice:** stickier than long grain; chewier

**Basmati rice:** nutty flavored, aromatic rice from India

**Arborio rice:** short-grain rice used in risotto

**Brown rice:** less processed than white rice, better for you

**Wild rice:** not really rice at all, but even less processed than brown rice, and even better for you

**Quinoa:** not rice either, but a grain from the Andes with small, disk-like seeds; extremely nutritious—check it out!

# French Fries

*Serves 1 to 2*

One of the most economical side dishes of all time.

*1 or 2 baking potatoes, peeled if desired*
*Oil*
*Salt*

Cut potatoes lengthwise in ⅜-inch wide strips or whatever size you prefer. Pour enough oil in the bottom of a large skillet or saucepan to completely cover, leaving no dry spots, and heat over medium-high until very hot. Carefully add the cut potatoes and fry until crisp and golden on all sides, about 7 to 8 minutes. Drain on paper towels. Just before serving, sprinkle with salt.

*veggie*

# Cheese-Stuffed Fried Tofu

*Serves 1 to 2*

1 (14- or 16-ounce) firm or extra-firm cake tofu, drained

2 slices (about 2 ounces) any favorite cheese

½ cup bread crumbs (I like to use Panko, sold in most Asian markets
   and now in most grocery stores too)

3 tablespoons Parmesan cheese (grated, shredded, or from the can)

Vegetable oil for frying

3 tablespoons all-purpose flour

1 egg, lightly beaten

Ranch dressing

Tomatoes

Drain all liquid from tofu and pat dry with paper towels. Cut tofu cake in half. Using a small paring knife, make a slit, lengthwise, leaving a border of ½ inch. Insert one slice of cheese in each slit. You may have to fold the cheese. Mix bread crumbs with Parmesan cheese. Heat a skillet over medium-high, adding enough oil to thoroughly coat the bottom. While the oil is heating, coat the tofu with flour, dip in the egg, then coat with bread crumb mixture. Using a spatula, transfer tofu cakes to hot oil. Fry on all sides until golden brown, about 5 minutes for each side. Serve with ranch dressing and fresh tomatoes.

# Stephanie's Barbecued Tofu

*Serves 1 to 2*

My neighbor Stephanie has given me many tofu recipes over the years, and this is our favorite.

*1 (14- or 16-ounce) firm cake tofu, drained*
*Vegetable oil for frying*
*½ cup barbecue sauce*
*1 tablespoon soy sauce*
*2 tablespoons sesame seeds*

Drain all liquid from tofu and pat dry with paper towels. Cut tofu cake into bite-sized pieces. Heat a skillet over medium-high, adding enough oil to completely coat the bottom thoroughly but lightly. When the oil is hot, add the tofu. Cook for 5 minutes. Using a spatula, turn tofu over. Add barbecue sauce, soy sauce, and sesame seeds. Continue cooking until tofu is crisp on each side, about 12 to 15 minutes. If barbecue sauce is too thick, add a little water to thin it out. Serve with rice. (See recipe for making rice in a microwave, page 149.)

# Fried Steak

*Serves 2*

The secret to a good steak is sealing in the juices with a well-heated skillet. Beware. You may set off your smoke alarm!

*2 steaks, such as strip, rib eye, or sirloin,*
    *about 1-inch thick*
*Salt and pepper*
*1 tablespoon butter or vegetable oil*

Heat a skillet for 5 minutes over medium heat. Sprinkle each side of each steak with salt and pepper.

Add butter or oil to the pan; swirl to coat the bottom. Add steaks, and cook until well browned on one side, about 5 minutes. Turn the steaks using tongs; cook 3 minutes more for rare, 4 minutes for medium-rare, or 5 minutes for medium. Remove steaks from pan. Great with tossed green salad and garlic bread.

# Sloppy Joes

*Serves 4*

1 pound ground beef
½ medium onion, chopped
½ teaspoon salt
1 teaspoon chili powder
1 teaspoon Worcestershire sauce
2 tablespoons brown sugar
1 (8-ounce) can tomato sauce
1 tablespoon vinegar
4 hamburger buns

In a large heavy skillet over medium heat, brown the ground beef and onions. Drain off and discard the grease; reduce heat to low. Add salt, chili powder, Worcestershire, brown sugar, tomato sauce, and vinegar. Cook about 7 minutes or until most of the liquid has evaporated. Serve on hamburger buns.

# Garlic-Herb Skillet Chicken

*Serves 2 to 4*

This dish is very economical if you buy a whole chicken and know how to cut it. I highly recommend using poultry shears or a pair of very good heavy-duty scissors for ease and safety.

1 2- to 3-pound chicken, cut up
1 teaspoon salt, or more to taste
1 teaspoon pepper, or more to taste
¼ cup (½ stick) butter or margarine
5 cloves garlic, minced
¼ cup chopped fresh parsley
2 tablespoons chopped fresh basil (optional; see Note)

Rinse chicken with cold water and pat dry with paper towels. Season with salt and pepper and set aside. Melt the butter in a large heavy frying pan or pot over medium heat. When butter has melted, add chicken skin-side down and fry until golden brown on the outside, about 10 minutes. Using a long-handled fork or a pair of tongs, turn chicken over. Add the garlic, and reduce the heat to low. Cover and cook about 1 hour, or until the chicken is very tender. Just before removing from the heat, add the parsley and basil, if using. Turn chicken over to coat with herbs. Serve over white rice if desired.

NOTE: *You could also use thyme, rosemary, or sage.*

# Smothered Pork Chops

*Serves 2 to 4*

1 tablespoon butter or vegetable-oil spray

4 large pork chops (about 1½ to 2 pounds), bone in

1 onion, coarsely chopped

1 (10½-ounce) can condensed cream of mushroom soup

1 teaspoon dried thyme

½ cup water

Applesauce (optional)

In a heavy skillet, over medium heat, melt butter (or spray with vegetable-oil cooking spray). Add pork chops and brown 2 minutes on each side. Transfer to a platter. Add onion to drippings in pan and cook 5 to 7 minutes, stirring frequently. Stir or whisk in soup, thyme, and water. Increase heat and bring to a boil. Return pork chops and any accumulated juices to pan. Reduce heat to medium-low, cover pan, and cook about 7 minutes, until pork is cooked through. Serve with applesauce, if desired.

# Curried Peanut Soup

*Serves 1 or 2*

I sometimes cut the broth back by 1 cup, substituting 1 cup of coconut milk. Either way, this soup is delightful.

*1 tablespoon peanut oil*
*1 small onion, sliced thin*
*1 garlic clove, minced*
*1 tablespoon, plus 1 teaspoon curry powder*
*1 (14-ounce) can chicken broth*
*¼ cup creamy peanut butter*
*1 teaspoon sugar*
*Chopped fresh cilantro, optional*

Heat oil in medium saucepan over medium heat. Add onion and sauté 5 minutes. Stir in garlic and curry powder and cook, stirring constantly, 1 or 2 minutes, or until garlic has lightly browned. Add stock and increase heat to medium high. Bring to a boil. Turn off heat and add peanut butter and sugar, stirring. When soup has cooled enough to handle, transfer to a blender and puree. (Can be prepared a day ahead and refrigerated.) Return puree to saucepan and stir over medium heat until heated through, thinning with more stock if preferred. Ladle soup into bowls and sprinkle with optional cilantro. Serve with white rice.

# Creamy Corn Chowder

*Serves 2 to 4*

*4 tablespoons butter or margarine*

*4 tablespoons all-purpose flour*

*2 cups milk*

*1 (14¾-ounce) can cream-style corn*

*½ cup red or green bell pepper, chopped very small*

*1 teaspoon ground cumin*

*1 teaspoon curry powder*

***Salt and pepper (optional)***

Melt butter in a large saucepan. Remove from heat and mix or whisk in flour until smooth. Slowly add milk, stirring or whisking constantly. Return pan to stove and cook on low heat until the milk starts to thicken. Stir corn into milk. The mixture should be at a gentle simmer. Do not boil. Add peppers, cumin, and curry, cooking until peppers are soft, about 5 minutes. Taste and adjust the seasons to your liking.

*veggie*

# Curried Sweet Potato Soup

*Serves 2 to 4*

This soup is easy, fast, and delicious. I often will add a touch of cream, milk, or half-and-half, if I have it, but it certainly isn't necessary.

1 (15-ounce) can sweet potato purée or sweetened pumpkin
1 (15-ounce) can chicken or vegetable broth
1 tablespoon curry powder

Combine all in a medium saucepan and warm on a medium heat, stirring constantly, until bubbling hot.

## Microwave
Combine all in a medium microwave-safe bowl. Microwave 3 minutes on full power.

# Miso Soup

*Serves 2 to 4*

4 cups water

4 tablespoons miso (soy bean paste)

1 (14- or 16-ounce) cake tofu, cut into small squares

2 green onions (scallions), thinly sliced

1 teaspoon sesame oil

Nori (dried seaweed) (optional)

In a large saucepan over a medium-high heat, bring water to a boil. Stir in miso until dissolved. Add tofu and simmer for 3 minutes. Stir in green onion slices, sesame oil, and nori, if using. Simmer for 10 minutes. Serve hot.

# Turkey Soup

Remember the turkey I mentioned in the beginning of the book? Well, after you have done all you can with it, make soup!

*1 turkey carcass with any leftover scraps*
*2 quarts (8 cups) water*
*2 carrots, sliced thick*
*1 onion, cut in quarters*
*2 or 3 stalks celery, sliced*
*1 teaspoon salt*
*Pepper, to taste*

Break up the turkey to fit into a large pot. Add the remaining ingredients and bring to a boil over a medium-high heat. Cover, reduce heat to a low simmer, and cook for about 2 hours. Serve hot with your favorite bread and butter.

For a heartier soup, add 1 cup uncooked rice during the last 20 minutes of cooking.

# 10.

# Microwave Marvels

Amicrowave is a safe and effective way to cook. Even though it's been around for a while, many people still don't know how it works. You might think it's obvious, you just put the food in and it heats up. But why does it heat the food and not the dish? And why does the inside of the oven stay cool? Microwave ovens produce electromagnetic radiation of exactly the right wavelength to excite water, fat, and sugar molecules. Since most of our food contains a fair amount of water, we can heat up our food by selectively heating up the water inside the food.

The microwave can be an important, and, to many, an indispensable appliance. While speed is its most obvious asset, it offers many other benefits as well. The interior never heats up, so it stays cool in the kitchen. It's very easy to clean. If food spatters, it can simply be wiped off with a damp cloth. It's convenient because you can heat and serve in the same utensil, be it a casserole, a plate, or a soup mug. And it's one of the safest appliances to use. That doesn't mean microwave accidents don't occur from time to time. Be safe and always use potholders when removing hot food from the microwave oven; the containers can get hot. Do not use metal containers in the microwave. In fact, avoid putting any sort of metal—from Chinese food containers to twist-ties—in the microwave. Glass is recommended because not all plastic and ceramic containers are safe and functional for the microwave. Food in round containers heats more evenly than square or rectangular containers. Microwave manufacturers recommend the following test to determine if your container is microwave-safe. Place 1 cup of room temperature water in container. Microwave on full power for 1 minute. Touch the container surface above the level of the water. If the container is hot, it is not recommended for use in the microwave. If the container is cool, it is acceptable for use in the microwave. Glass that is too thin might not withstand high temperatures and may crack.

Most foods should be covered when being cooked in the microwave. Not only will covering the food keep the heat and moisture in, but it also keeps the oven clean too.

Once a week or so, clean your microwave by tossing a small wet towel inside, closing the door and heating for 1 minute on full power. The wet towel will release steam and dried foods will wipe off more easily.

## MICROWAVE BASICS

- Food molecules continue to vibrate and produce heat in microwaved foods after they are out of the oven. Let the food stand before being eaten.
- In a microwave, the food nearest the outside of the dish cooks most rapidly. Remember this when arranging food in a cooking dish. For best results, place the thickest parts of the food toward the outside. If cooking two different vegetables, such as carrots and broccoli, place the longer-cooking item (the carrots) around the edge and the shorter-cooking item (the broccoli) in the center.
- Select dishes that just hold the food and that have some depth. Cooking in a dish too large will affect the success of a recipe and a dish too shallow can cause spillovers.
- You will notice that in most recipes we recommend covering the cooking dishes tightly. Foods requiring steam to cook will need tight covers.
- To prevent spattering of food that doesn't need covering, such as bacon, use a plain white paper towel or paper plate as a cover.

## Scrambled eggs

cooked in the microwave turn out fluffy and are a cinch to make. Simply place 1 or 2 tea-spoons of butter in a 2-cup glass measure. Microwave about 30 seconds on full power until the butter has melted. Break 2 eggs into the cup and add 1 to 2 tablespoons milk. Mix with fork to scramble eggs. Microwave 1 minute at full power. With a fork, break up cooked portions and stir them to the center. Microwave 30 seconds longer. The eggs will not be completely set. Let stand 1 to 3 minutes to complete cooking.

## Bacon

will cook crisp and brown in the microwave. Arrange 3 slices of bacon on three layers of paper towels. Cover with 1 layer of paper towel. Microwave 2 to 3 minutes on full power. Al-low bacon to cool slightly before removing.

## Baked potatoes

turn out great cooked in the microwave. As previously mentioned, foods continue to cook after they are removed from the oven. If you cook the potato until it feels soft, it will be over-cooked by serving time. For the best results, microwave one medium potato for 4 to 5 minutes at full power, remove from oven, wrap in foil, and let stand for 10 to 15 minutes. The potato will actually stay hot for up to 30 minutes.

## Artichokes

are ready in minutes! Trim off the stem and 1 inch off the top. Wrap in waxed paper and cook on full power for 6 minutes for each.

## Rice

is a cinch in the microwave. Combine 1 cup rice, 2 cups water, and 1 tablespoon butter or margarine in 2- to 3-quart deep microwave-safe casserole. Cover and cook on full power 5 min-utes or until boiling. Reduce setting to half power and cook 15 minutes.

## Frozen vegetables

come out tender-crisp cooked in the microwave. Place a single serving (about 1 cup) of your favorite vegetables in a serving dish. Cover tightly with plastic wrap. Microwave 3 to 4 minutes on full power. Use caution when removing the plastic wrap because of steam.

## Oatmeal

will be ready in a flash cooked in the microwave. Combine ⅓ cup of quick-cooking oats (not instant) with ¾ cup of water in a serving bowl. Cover and cook at full power for 2 minutes and 30 seconds. Let stand 1 minute.

## S'Mores

are much easier in a microwave than they are at a campfire! Place a graham cracker on a paper towel or plate and top with a piece of chocolate and a marshmallow. Microwave on full power for 20 to 30 seconds or until the marshmallow starts to expand. Let stand 20 seconds.

# Steamed Chicken

This chicken is super easy and is wonderful served over white rice.

*1 small whole chicken (about 2 pounds)*
*3 tablespoons soy sauce*
*1 small onion, peeled*

Place chicken, breast side up, in a deep microwave-safe baking dish. Brush cavity and outside of chicken with soy sauce. Stuff onion into chicken cavity. Cover tightly. Microwave on full power for 10 minutes. Remove and turn chicken over. Re-cover and microwave on full power 10 minutes more. Let stand, covered 10 minutes. Always make sure the chicken is no longer pink before serving.

### Variation
For a sweeter flavor, you can add ¼ cup orange juice to the soy sauce before cooking.

# Garlic Chicken

*Serves 2 to 4*

Garlic cooked this way is sweet and mild. Serve this dish with bread and use the softened garlic as your "butter."

> 4 to 8 smaller chicken pieces (about 1½ to 2 pounds)
> ¼ cup olive oil
> 1 teaspoon salt
> 1 teaspoon pepper
> 12 to 14 cloves garlic, with or without the skins
>     (about 1 head, broken up)

Place chicken in a deep microwave-safe casserole with a tight-fitting lid. Pour the olive oil over chicken, mixing with your hands to coat the chicken pieces evenly. Sprinkle the salt and pepper over the chicken and mix again. Add the garlic cover and microwave on full power for 10 minutes. At this point, if you don't have a turntable, you must turn the baking dish half a turn. Continue cooking for 8 minutes more. Let stand, covered, 15 minutes. Always make sure the chicken is no longer pink before serving. If you cooked the garlic with the skin on, squeeze out the garlic and discard the skins. Serve with any green vegetable.

# Orange-Glazed Chicken

*Serves 4*

*2 pounds chicken pieces (about 8 pieces)*
*½ cup orange marmalade*
*¼ cup orange juice*
*2 tablespoons cornstarch*
*2 tablespoons packed brown sugar*
*2 tablespoons lemon juice*
*1 teaspoon salt*
*½ orange, peeled, sliced, and quartered*

In a 4-quart or larger microwave-safe casserole or a large glass baking dish, arrange chicken with thickest parts to the outside. Cover with lid or plastic wrap and microwave on full power for 15 minutes. Mix marmalade, orange juice, cornstarch, brown sugar, lemon juice, and salt in 2-quart microwave-safe bowl. (Pyrex glass measures are perfect for this.) Spoon in juices from the cooked chicken. Microwave sauce uncovered on full power for 3 minutes. If sauce is not boiling and thick, continue to cook 1 minute more. Stir in orange slices and spoon sauce over chicken. Cover chicken loosely to avoid spatters and microwave on full power for 10 minutes or until chicken is no longer pink. Let stand 10 minutes to complete cooking. Serve with your favorite rice dish.

# Chicken and Rice Casserole

*Serves 4*

1 cup uncooked rice

1 (10½-ounce) can any "cream of" soup

1 (4-ounce) can sliced mushrooms

1 cup water

2 pounds chicken pieces (thighs and drumsticks work best)
   (about 8 pieces)

In a 4-quart or larger microwave-safe casserole or a large glass baking dish, combine rice, soup, mushrooms, and water. Top with chicken pieces. Cover with lid or plastic wrap. Cook on full power 10 minutes. Rotate pan. Continue cooking on full power for 12 more minutes or until rice is tender and chicken is no longer pink. Serve with spinach or other green vegetable.

# Steak Cordon Bleu

*Serves 2*

*4- to 6½-ounce spreadable cheese with garlic and herbs*
  *(found near the cream cheese in the grocer's refrigerator aisle)*
*2 (4 ounces each) beef cube steaks*
*2 thin slices ham*
*1 thin slice Swiss cheese, cut in half crosswise*

Spread a thin layer of cheese on each cubed steak. Top with a ham slice. Spread the ham with remaining cheese. Place Swiss cheese on top and roll up.

Place steaks in a small glass baking dish with seam-side down to keep steaks from opening. Cover with plastic wrap and microwave at full power for 3 minutes. Remove from oven, rearrange for even cooking, re-cover, and continue cooking at the DEFROST (30 percent power) setting 4 to 5 minutes or until the meat is done and no longer pink. Let stand, covered, 5 minutes. This is a rich dish, so serve with a light side dish like snap peas or green beans.

# Stuffed Peppers

*Serves 2 to 4*

*4 green peppers, tops, core, and seeds removed*
*¾ pound ground beef*
*1 small onion, minced*
*1 cup rice, uncooked*
*1½ cups tomato sauce*
*1½ cups water*

Place peppers in a deep microwave-safe casserole with lid. Combine remaining ingredients in a mixing bowl and stuff peppers all the way to the tops. Cover and cook at full power for 15 minutes or until peppers are tender and filling is firm. Let stand, covered, 5 minutes. Serve with a tossed green salad.

# Cheesy Meat Loaf

*Serves 2 to 4*

1 pound ground beef
3 slices of bread, moistened with water
1 egg
1 small onion, chopped
¼ cup barbecue sauce or ketchup
1 tablespoon Worcestershire sauce
¼ cup Parmesan cheese (grated, shredded, or from the can)

With your hands, combine beef, bread, egg, onion, barbecue sauce, and Worcestershire in a large bowl. Pat down into a microwave-safe baking ring. Sprinkle with Parmesan cheese. Cover with waxed paper and cook on full power for 8 minutes or until set and firm. Let stand for 5 minutes.

# Beef Stroganoff with Buttered Noodles

*Serves 2 to 4*

*2 cups beef cubes (about 1 pound)*

*1 cup beef broth*

*½ cup sliced mushrooms, fresh or canned*

　　*(more if you really like mushrooms)*

*1 cup sour cream*

*2 tablespoons all-purpose flour*

Combine beef, broth, and mushrooms in a deep microwave-safe casserole with lid. Cook at full power for 6 minutes. Mix together sour cream and flour and add to meat. Cook on full power 2 minutes. Stir until thick. Serve over buttered noodles.

BUTTERED NOODLES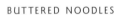

*6 ounces dry noodles (egg noodles work best, but you*

　　*could also use penne, macaroni, or shells)*

*2 or 3 tablespoons butter*

Cook noodles according to package microwave instructions, or place noodles in 4 quarts of water in a large microwave-safe bowl and microwave on full power for 10 minutes. Drain and add butter. Toss until the butter has coated all the noodles. Serve with peas or other green vegetable.

# Salmon in Lettuce

*Serves 2*

I won First Place in a microwave cooking contest with this recipe. It was given to me by Penny Berglas. Thanks, Penny!

2 salmon fillets (8 ounces each)
1 teaspoon salt
2 large lettuce leaves
1 small onion, sliced thin
2 tablespoons balsamic vinegar
2 tablespoons honey

Sprinkle the salmon fillets with the salt. Wrap each fillet in a lettuce leaf. Place the onions in the bottom of a microwave-safe casserole with a tight fitting lid. Place the lettuce-wrapped salmon on top of the onions. Pour the vinegar and honey over all. Cover and cook on full power for about 8 minutes, or until the salmon has cooked through. This low-fat dish goes well with rice.

# Bacon and Eggs Creamy Casserole

*Serves 4*

4 slices bacon

1 (12-ounce) package frozen hash browns
   (or ½ of 28-ounce package)

6 eggs

⅓ cup heavy cream

1 cup shredded cheese, your choice

2 tablespoons chopped chives (optional)

Lay out bacon in a shallow microwave-safe dish, cover with a paper towel, and cook for 4 minutes. Remove and let cool; crumble and set aside. Place hash browns in a 2-quart covered microwave-safe casserole and cook on full power for 7 minutes. Meanwhile, combine eggs, cream, cheese, and reserved crumbled bacon. Pour over cooked hash browns and stir lightly. Return to microwave and cook on full power 4 minutes. Remove and stir. Continue cooking until eggs have almost set, checking every 30 seconds. Sprinkle in chives. Let stand, covered, 5 minutes. Serve with sliced tomatoes.

# French-Style Potatoes

*Serves 2*

*½ cup (1 stick) butter or margarine*
*½ teaspoon paprika*
*4 baking potatoes, peeled and thinly sliced*
*1 teaspoon salt*
*Black pepper*

Place ¼ cup (½ stick) butter and paprika in a round microwave-safe dish. Microwave on full power for 1 minute. Swirl melted butter to thoroughly coat dish. Layer potato slices evenly in dish. Slice remaining butter into pats and place evenly over potatoes. Sprinkle with salt and pepper. Cover tightly. Microwave on full power 10 minutes. Let stand, covered, 5 minutes.

## Variation
Sprinkle any grated cheese over potatoes just before serving.

# Glazed Carrots

*Serves 2*

*4 carrots, peeled, thinly sliced*

*2 tablespoons butter or margarine*

*1 teaspoon sugar*

*¼ cup orange juice*

Combine all ingredients in a microwave-safe bowl. Cover tightly. Cook on full power for 4 minutes. Remove and stir; re-cover and cook 2 minutes longer. Keep covered and let stand for 5 minutes.

*veggie*

# Baked Green Beans

*Serves 2*

1 (10-ounce) package frozen green beans, any type
1 (10½-ounce) can condensed cream of mushroom soup
¼ cup milk
1 (2½-ounce) can fried onion rings

Combine green beans, soup, and milk in a microwave-safe 2-quart or larger casserole. Cover and cook on full power for 9 minutes. Stir in all but a tablespoon or two of the onion rings. Cook on full power 2 minutes. Garnish with reserved onion rings.

# Scrumptious Baked Beans

*Serves 2 to 4*

4 slices bacon

1 cup ketchup

2 (15-ounce) cans any favorite beans, drained (kidney beans,
    red beans, butter beans, black beans, rinsed)

½ cup brown sugar

1 tablespoon prepared mustard

1 tablespoon Worcestershire sauce

Place bacon in a microwave-safe 2-quart casserole and cover with a paper towel. Cook for 4 minutes. Remove bacon and when cooled, crumble. Stir the remaining ingredients into bacon drippings, along with the crumbled bacon. Cover and cook on full power for 7 minutes.

# Parmesan Zucchini

*Serves 2*

*3 medium zucchini, thinly sliced*

*2 tablespoons butter or margarine*

*¼ cup Parmesan cheese (grated, shredded, or from the can)*

Place zucchini in a microwave-safe bowl. Dot all over with butter. Cover tightly. Microwave on full power for 3 minutes. Remove cover and sprinkle with Parmesan cheese. Re-cover and let stand 5 minutes before serving.

# Sesame Snow Peas

*Serves 1 to 2*

6 ounces fresh or frozen (thawed) snow peas
1 teaspoon vegetable oil
1 teaspoon sesame seeds
½ teaspoon sesame oil
Salt and pepper

Toss together peas, vegetable oil, sesame seeds, and sesame oil in a microwave-safe bowl. Cover with plastic wrap, pulling back one corner to vent. Cook on full power 1 minute for crisp-tender, 2 minutes for tender. Go light on the salt and pepper.

# Creamy Noodles

*Serves 1 to 2*

½ *of a 10-ounce package egg noodles*
1 *(10½-ounce) can condensed cream of mushroom soup*
*Salt and pepper*

Cook noodles according to package microwave instructions, or place noodles in 4 quarts of water in a large microwave-safe bowl and microwave on full power for 10 minutes. Drain water and return noodles to warm dish. Add soup and mix well. Salt and pepper to taste. Add a little water or milk if you find the noodles too thick for your taste. Return to microwave and heat on full power 1 minute. Serve warm.

*veggie*

# Classic Fettuccine

*Serves 2 to 4*

*8 ounces fettuccine noodles*
*½ cup (1 stick) butter*
*½ cup heavy cream, slightly warm*
*½ cup grated Parmesan cheese, plus extra for serving*
*1 teaspoon pepper, or more to taste*
*1 egg yolk*

Cook the noodles *al dente* according to the package microwave instructions. Drain and set aside. In a large glass microwave-safe casserole, melt the butter on full power for 1 minute. Add the cooked noodles and toss. Stir in the cream, cheese, and pepper. Cook 20 seconds on full power. While still very hot, add the egg yolk and toss quickly until all is well-blended. Serve immediately with extra Parmesan cheese. Goes great with tossed green salad and garlic bread.

# MICROWAVE MELTS

Easy to assemble, quick to heat, and tasty to eat, melts make the best lunches and snacks. Use any amount of the ingredients to individualize your own creations.

## Quick Pizza

*Serves 1*

1 English muffin, split, preferably toasted
Pepperoni slices
Canned pizza sauce or marinara sauce
Provolone or mozzarella cheese
Dash of dried oregano (less than ⅛ teaspoon)

Place the split muffin cut-side up on a plate. Top with pepperoni, sauce, cheese, and oregano. Heat on full power for 1 minute. Let stand 1 minute.

# Reuben Melt

*Serves 1*

*2 slices of rye bread, preferably toasted*
*Thinly sliced corned beef or pastrami*
*Shredded Swiss cheese*
*Sauerkraut*
*Thousand Island dressing*

Place one slice of bread on a plate. In a bowl, combine the corned beef, cheese, sauerkraut, and dressing and spoon onto bread. Top with remaining slice of bread. Heat on full power for about 1 minute or until cheese melts. Let stand for 1 minute.

# Turkey and Swiss Melt

*Serves 1*

**2 slices rye or black bread**
**Russian dressing**
**Turkey slices**
**Thinly sliced Swiss cheese**

Place the bread on a plate. Spread the dressing over each slice. Top one slice with turkey, cheese, and remaining slice of bread. Heat on full power for 1 minute or until cheese melts. Let stand for 1 minute.

# Quesadillas

*Serves 1*

**2 flour tortillas**
**Shredded cheddar or jack cheese**
**Chopped jalapeño peppers**
**Sour cream**

Place 1 tortilla on a paper towel or plate. Top with cheese and jalapeño peppers. Place other tortilla on top. Heat on full power for 1 minute or until cheese has melted. Remove and allow to cool slightly. Cut into wedges. Dip in sour cream.

## Variation
To make nachos, substitute tortilla chips for the flour tortillas.

## TRISCUIT MELTS

Triscuit Baked Whole Wheat Wafers are THE answer to severe cases of snack attacks. In each of the following recipes, microwave 6 at a time for 30 seconds, or until the cheese melts.

### Crab Canapes

Mix 6 ounces of canned crab meat (rinsed and drained) with ½ cup mayonnaise, ¼ cup shredded cheese, 2 tablespoons of chopped green onion, and ½ teaspoon of Worcestershire sauce.

### Cheddar Munchies

Place cheddar cheese, cooked cocktail hot dog, and a dab of mustard on a Triscuit.

### Nachos Supreme

Top Triscuits with sliced cheddar cheese, prepared salsa, sour cream, and slices of jalapeño peppers.

### Manly Man Chili

Top Triscuits with fiery hot chili and sprinkling of shredded cheddar cheese.

*veggie*

# Hot and Spicy Cream Cheese

Mix 1 spoonful of hot prepared horseradish, 1 spoonful of apricot jam, and 3 heaping spoonfuls of cream cheese together. Heat for 30 seconds or just until warmed. Spoon over Triscuits.

# Hot Chocolate

*Serves 4*

3 tablespoons unsweetened cocoa powder

3 tablespoons sugar

4 cups milk

Whipped cream or mini-marshmallows

In a large microwave-safe bowl, combine cocoa powder, sugar, and milk. Microwave on full power for 8 minutes. Stir until chocolate is completely dissolved. Microwave 2 minutes more. Pour into mugs. Top with whipped cream or marshmallows.

# Vanilla Custard Ice Cream

*Serves 4 to 6*

The affordable mini electric ice cream freezers require very little effort to make homemade ice cream treats. Basically you just plug them in. You can find the freezers in kitchen stores for about $30.

*2 cups milk*

*2 eggs*

*¾ cup sugar*

*1 tablespoon vanilla extract*

*1 cup heavy cream*

In a large microwave-safe bowl, combine milk, eggs, and sugar, beating well with a rotary beater or whisk. Microwave on full power for 6 minutes, stirring or whisking every 2 minutes to prevent lumps. Allow to cool a few minutes. Blend in vanilla and cream. Pour into ice cream freezer and process.

*veggie*

# Nutty-Caramel Cinnamon Buns

*Serves 4*

3 tablespoons butter

⅓ cup brown sugar

1 tablespoon water

1 teaspoon ground cinnamon

⅓ cup chopped nuts

1 can (8 or 10 count) refrigerator biscuits, each cut in half

In a round microwave-safe baking pan, combine the butter, sugar, water, cinnamon, and nuts. Cook on full power for 1 minute. Stir to mix. Coat each biscuit in mixture. Place in pan with sides slightly touching. Cook on full power for 2 minutes. Rotate the pan and continue cooking 1 minute on half power. Be careful, nuts will be very hot.

# No-Bake Corn Flake Cookies

*Yields 2 dozen*

**1 cup butterscotch chips**
**½ cup peanut butter**
**2 cups corn flakes**

Line a cookie sheet with waxed paper. In a 2-quart microwave-safe bowl, combine butterscotch chips and peanut butter. Microwave on full power for 2 minutes. Remove and stir until smooth. Stir in corn flakes. Drop the cookie mixture by teaspoonful onto cookie sheet while still warm. Reshape cookies when cooled off a bit.

*veggie*

# Rocky Road

*Yields 1 ½ pounds*

*Butter for greasing dish*
*1 (12-ounce) package semisweet chocolate chips*
*1 ounce (1 square) unsweetened baking chocolate,*
    *broken into pieces*
*3 tablespoons solid vegetable shortening*
*12 to 13 large marshmallows*
*1 cup whole roasted unsalted almonds*

Prepare a deep baking dish (a 9 × 5-inch loaf pan works great) by greasing well or lining with wax or parchment paper. In a 1-quart microwave-safe container, combine ⅓ of the chocolate chips, ⅓ of the unsweetened chocolate, and 1 tablespoon vegetable shortening. Microwave on full power for 30 seconds. Remove and stir until smooth. If chocolate hasn't melted entirely, return to the microwave for 10 seconds on high. Pour into prepared dish. Sprinkle with half of the marshmallows and half of the nuts. Repeat above, again using ⅓ of each of the chocolates and 1 tablespoon shortening. Cover with remaining marshmallows and nuts, and top with final layer of chocolate and shortening mixture. Chill until very firm. Cut into large pieces to serve.

# II.

# The Slow Cooker

What could be better than a meal that practically cooks by itself? Slow cookers or Crock-Pots—brand name known to most—are safe when used according to the manufacturer's instructions. Always use pot holders when moving a hot slow cooker, and be careful to place the cord so it will not hang over the counter where it can be touched accidentally.

# Very Basic Slow-Cooked Chicken

*Serves 2*

After cooking, you'll have tender, moist, delicious chicken that can be eaten alone or used as a base for sandwiches, salads, burritos, and enchiladas. (For example, see Cheesy Chicken Enchiladas on page 115.)

*1 whole small chicken, about 2 pounds*
*1 teaspoon garlic salt*

Rinse chicken and if desired, remove the skin. Sprinkle garlic salt all over chicken and place in slow cooker. Don't add any liquids. Cover and cook on low for 7 to 8 hours.

# Teriyaki Chicken

*Serves 2*

**4 chicken breasts (you can use skinless, boneless ones if desired)**
**¼ cup teriyaki sauce**

Rinse chicken, pat dry with paper towels, and place in slow cooker. Pour teriyaki sauce over the chicken, cover, and cook on low for 7 to 8 hours. Yummy over rice.

# Honey-Mustard Chicken

*Serves 2 to 3*

1 small whole chicken, about 2 pounds
½ cup orange juice
¼ cup honey
¼ cup sweet-and-tangy mustard
1 teaspoon garlic salt
1 teaspoon curry powder

Rinse and pat dry chicken. Place in slow cooker. Mix the orange juice, honey, mustard, salt, and curry and pour over the chicken. Cook on low for 10 hours. Serve hot. Great over rice.

# Crock-Pot BBQ Ribs

*Serves 2 to 4*

A Puente family favorite for twenty years.

*2 to 4 pounds spareribs, or any favorite rib*
*1 medium onion, sliced*
*2 cups of your favorite barbecue sauce*

Combine all ingredients in the slow cooker and cook on low for 7 hours, or until the meat falls away from the bone. Add water if your sauce is too thick. Serve with baked or mashed potatoes.

# Crock-Pot Brisket

*Serves 4*

**3 pounds brisket in one piece**
**1 envelope onion soup mix**

Place brisket in the slow cooker and top with onion soup mix. Do not add any liquid. Cook on low for 8 hours. Serve with Glazed Carrots (page 162).

# 12.

# Crunchy, Chewy, Gooey, Nutty, and Crumbly Desserts

From time to time, we all crave something sweet. Here are tips to help you become a better baker and dessert maker.

Unless otherwise stated, always use unsalted butter (also known as sweet butter) in baking. Salt is usually in the ingredients, so salted butter adds extra salt to the recipe. If you were using salted butter, you must subtract the amount of salt in the butter. It's much easier to use unsalted. Margarine may be substituted for butter, but butter produces a much better flavor.

Eggs come in different sizes and in most cases it's best to use large.

Oatmeal comes in different varieties. Use quick-cooking (3 to 5 minutes). Do not use slow-cooking or instant.

Unless otherwise indicated, when a recipe calls for sugar, use granulated white. When a recipe calls for brown sugar, always pack it into the cup.

Bake cookies and most fruit desserts on the middle rack of the oven so the heat circulates evenly. Preheating the oven is very important. Always preheat for at least 15 minutes before baking.

*veggie*

# Twinkie Dessert

### (Or Yikes! Company's coming and we have nothing to serve)

*Serves 4 to 6*

1 (15-ounce) box Twinkies

1 large carton (16-ounces) frozen strawberries
   or any favorite berries (frozen with sugar)

1 (8-ounce) tub frozen whipped topping

Split the Twinkies lengthwise and lay them out, creme side up, in a 9 × 13-inch pan. Thaw berries and pour, juice and all, over the Twinkies. Spread the topping over all. Chill until ready to serve.

*veggie*

# Cheesecake

*Serves 4*

1 ready-made graham cracker crust

2 eggs, beaten

1 cup sour cream

2 (8-ounce) packages cream cheese, at room temperature

½ cup sugar

½ teaspoon vanilla extract

Preheat oven to 375°F. In a large bowl, using an electric mixer, combine eggs, sour cream, cream cheese, sugar, and vanilla. Pour into crust. Bake for 50 minutes. Cool before serving.

# Cake Mix Cookies

*Yields 2 dozen cookies*

**1 box cake mix, any flavor**

**2 eggs**

**½ cup vegetable cooking oil**

**½ cup of any of the following: chopped walnuts, pecans, hazelnuts,
  almonds, macadamia nuts, chocolate chips**

Preheat oven to 350°F. Mix all ingredients in a large bowl until blended. Drop spoonfuls of batter on a nonstick cookie sheet 2 inches apart. Bake for 9 to 10 minutes or until the cookies have set but are still a little soft in the center. Serve warm if desired. Cookies will firm up when cool.

NOTE: *These cookies will stay fresh-tasting for up to a week if stored in an airtight container at room temperature.*

# Peanut Butter Cookies

*Yields 1 dozen cookies*

Honestly, these are really good!

   *1 cup sugar*
   *1 cup chunky peanut butter*
   *1 egg*

Preheat oven to 350°F. In a medium bowl, combine the sugar, peanut butter, and egg. Drop a spoonful at a time on a cookie sheet. Press with a fork to make ridges on the tops of the cookies. Bake for 12 minutes. Serve warm. Store cookies in an airtight container in a cool, dry area.

*veggie*

# Peanut Butter 'n Honey Cookies

*Yields 2 dozen cookies*

¾ *cup honey*

¼ *cup (½ stick) butter, softened*

1 *egg*

¾ *cup peanut butter*

1 *teaspoon pure vanilla extract*

1½ *cups all-purpose flour, plus extra for shaping*

½ *teaspoon salt*

½ *teaspoon baking soda*

*Butter or vegetable-oil spray, for greasing cookie sheet*

Preheat oven to 350°F. In medium bowl, beat honey and butter until light and fluffy. Beat in egg, peanut butter, and vanilla. Add flour, salt, and baking soda; mix just until combined. Avoid overbeating. Drop dough, one tablespoon at a time, on greased cookie sheet. Dip a fork into flour and press flat on each cookie to form ridges. Bake for 10 to 12 minutes or until golden. Cool before serving. Store in airtight container in a cool, dry area.

# Peanut Butter Fudge

*Yields 12 squares*

1 (12-ounce) package of butterscotch, or chocolate chips
1 cup creamy or crunchy peanut butter
1 (14-ounce) can sweetened condensed milk
  (not evaporated milk)

Line a 9-inch square pan with waxed paper. Place the chips and peanut butter in a small saucepan. Over a low heat, stirring constantly, heat until soft and melted. Remove from heat and add condensed milk. Pour mixture into prepared pan. Allow to cool before cutting and serving. Store fudge in an airtight container in a cool, dry area.

# Peanut Brittle

*Yields about 1 pound*

Although this recipe is easy to do, please be aware that the mixture becomes extremely hot. Use caution and pay close attention to what you are doing at all times.

> 1 cup sugar
>
> ½ cup light corn syrup
>
> ¼ cup water
>
> 1 tablespoon butter
>
> 1 cup roasted salted peanuts
>
> 1 teaspoon vanilla extract
>
> 2 teaspoons baking soda

Line two cookie sheets with waxed paper and set aside. (If you don't have waxed paper, you can butter your cookie sheets.) In a medium saucepan, mix sugar, corn syrup, and water. Over medium-high heat, stirring constantly with a wooden spoon, bring mixture to a boil. Continue boiling for 10 minutes or until mixture reaches 260°F on a candy thermometer. Add butter and peanuts. Lower heat to medium-low. Stir and cook until a light golden color, about 5 minutes. Don't burn the peanuts!

Remove from heat and add vanilla. Add baking soda—look out for foaming, frothing, and expanding. Pour onto cookie sheets. Using oven mitts to hold cookie sheets, tilt sheets to level mixture. Cool completely, then break into pieces. Store in airtight container.

# Walnut-Butter Cookies

*Yields 2 to 3 dozen cookies*

1¾ cups all-purpose flour
⅓ cup sugar
1¼ cups ground walnuts (see Note)
2 eggs
1 cup (2 sticks) butter
Butter for greasing cookie sheet
Confectioners' sugar (optional)

Preheat oven to 350°F. In a large bowl, mix flour, sugar, and ground walnuts. Make a small well in the flour mixture and add egg yolks. Cut butter into small pieces and add to the flour mixture. Mix by hand and shape into a ball. If dough is sticky, add a small amount of flour. When all ingredients are well combined, form into 1-inch balls, rolling in the palm of your hand. Place cookies 1 inch apart on a greased baking sheet. Bake 10 minutes until lightly browned. If desired, roll the warm cookies in confectioners' sugar after you remove from oven. Allow to cool before serving. Store cookies in an airtight container in a cool, dry area.

NOTE: *Walnuts can be ground in a mini food processor, blender, or coffee bean grinder.*

*veggie*

# Shortbread Cookies

*Yields 2 dozen cookies*

These cookies simply melt in your mouth. You'll love them!

*1 cup butter, plus extra for greasing pan*
*½ cup confectioners' sugar*
*2 cups flour*
*¼ teaspoon salt*

Preheat oven to 300°F. Lightly grease a 9-inch square baking pan. Cream together butter and sugar. Add flour and salt and mix into a stiff dough. Press dough into pan. Prick top with a fork and bake for 30 minutes, or until a light golden brown color. Remove from oven, cool slightly, and slice into small squares. Store cookies in an airtight container.

# Pecan Cookies

*Yields 2 dozen cookies*

**1 cup (2 sticks) butter, slightly softened**
**½ cup confectioners' sugar, plus 1 tablespoon for dusting**
**1 teaspoon vanilla extract**
**1¾ cup all-purpose flour**
**1 cup chopped pecans or walnuts**

Using an electric mixer, beat butter until creamy. Beat in sugar and vanilla. Beat for 5 minutes, or until mixture is fluffy. For a light and airy cookie, gently stir in flour and nuts. Chill 2 hours. Preheat oven to 350°F. Shape dough into 24 bite-sized balls. Place 1 inch apart on cookie sheet. Bake 10 to 12 minutes. Remove the cookies from oven and dust with powdered sugar. Allow to cool before serving. Store cookies in an airtight container in a cool dry area.

*veggie*

# Fruit and Oat Bars

*Yields 12 large bars*

The perfect dessert to take to a potluck party or share with your friends.

*1½ cups all-purpose flour*

*1 cup brown sugar, firmly packed*

*1 teaspoon salt*

*2 cups quick-cooking oatmeal*

*1 cup (2 sticks) butter, cut into pats about 1 tablespoon each*
  *(8 pats per stick), plus extra for greasing pan*

*1½ cups seedless raspberry, strawberry, or apricot jam*

*½ cup chopped pecans*

Preheat oven to 375°F. In a large bowl, combine flour, sugar, salt, and oatmeal. Add all but 2 pats of butter into mixture; blend with a fork. Press half of oatmeal mixture evenly into a greased 9 × 13-inch pan. Spread jam over batter in pan, top with remaining oatmeal mixture. Dot with remaining two tablespoons butter; sprinkle with chopped pecans. Bake for 20 to 25 minutes. Let cool completely. Cut into 12 bars. Store oat bars in an airtight container in a cool, dry area.

# Classic Cookie Bars

¼ cup (½ stick) butter, melted

1 cup graham cracker crumbs

1 cup shredded coconut

1 cup chocolate chips

1 cup chopped pecans

1 (14-ounce) can sweetened condensed milk

Vanilla ice cream (optional)

Preheat oven to 350°F. Pour melted butter in the bottom of a 9-inch square pan. Sprinkle on one layer each of the graham cracker crumbs, coconut, chocolate chips, and pecans. Pour the sweetened condensed milk over the top, and bake for 30 minutes. The edges should be slightly browned. When completely cooled, cut into squares. If you dare, serve warm and gooey from the oven with vanilla ice cream. Store cookie bars in an airtight container in a cool, dry area.

# Date Bars

*Yields 16 squares*

Easy—no baking!

1 cup pitted dates
2 cups pecans or walnuts
1 cup raisins
8 ounces dried figs
Butter for greasing pan

Combine all ingredients in a food processor until finely chopped. Firmly press into a well-greased 8-inch square baking pan and cut into squares. Store date bars in an airtight container in a cool, dry area.

*veggie*

# Apricot Drops

*Yields 2 dozen cookies*

1¼ cup all-purpose flour

¼ cup sugar

1 teaspoon baking powder

¼ teaspoon salt

1 (3-ounce) package cream cheese, softened

½ cup (1 stick) butter or margarine, softened

1 cup apricot jam (or your favorite flavor fruit jam)

Preheat oven to 350°F. In a large mixing bowl, combine flour, sugar, baking powder, and salt. Using a fork to mix, add cream cheese and butter, a little at a time, until mixture is crumbly. Add ½ cup jam, mixing well. Drop by spoonfuls on cookie sheet. Bake 10 to 12 minutes. Remove from oven and when cookies are cool, spread them with remaining jam. Store in an airtight container in a cool, dry area.

# No-Bake Chocolate Crunchies

*Yields 2 dozen cookies*

This recipe can also be done using the microwave oven to melt the chocolate chips. Use full power and check for melting every 30 seconds by using a wooden spoon.

1 (6-ounce) package semi-sweet chocolate chips
½ cup peanut butter
1 (3-ounce) can chow mein or rice noodles
1 cup roasted salted peanuts

In a small saucepan, combine chocolate chips and peanut butter. Heat over very low heat, stirring constantly, until chips are melted. Add chow mein noodles and peanuts, stirring until well-combined. Remove from heat and drop by spoonfuls onto waxed paper. Allow to cool before serving. Store in an airtight container in a cool, dry area.

# Peanut Butter and Chocolate Crispy Treats

*Yields 6 large squares*

As in the Chocolate Crunchies recipe, you may use the microwave oven to melt the chocolate chips.

> 1 cup sugar
> 1 cup light corn syrup
> 1 cup peanut butter
> 6 cups crispy rice cereal
> Butter for greasing pan
> 1 cup semisweet chocolate chips

Combine sugar and corn syrup in a large pot. Cook over medium heat until bubbly and sugar has dissolved. Remove from heat and stir in peanut butter. Mix well. Add cereal and stir until well-blended. Press into a buttered 9 × 13-inch pan. Melt chips over very low heat or in the microwave. Spread over cereal mixture. Let cool and cut into 6 squares. Store in an airtight container in a cool, dry area.

# Classic Yellow Cake with Easy Orange Glaze

*Serves 8 to 10*

¾ cup (1½ sticks) butter, softened,

    plus extra for greasing pans

1½ cups sugar

2 cups all-purpose flour

2 teaspoons baking powder

¼ teaspoon salt

3 eggs

1 egg yolk

¾ cup milk

2 teaspoons vanilla extract

Prepare two 9-inch diameter round pans or one 9 × 13 × 2-inch pan: butter and line the bottoms with parchment or waxed paper. Set a rack at the middle level of the oven and pre-heat to 350°F.

In a large bowl, beat butter and sugar with an electric mixer about 5 minutes, until light and fluffy. In a small bowl, stir together flour, baking powder, and salt; set aside. Combine eggs, egg yolk, milk, and vanilla extract in a 2-cup measuring cup. Add ⅓ of the flour mixture to butter mixture, half the milk mixture, mixing to blend after each addition. Continue to alternate, beginning and ending with flour mixture. Scrape down bowl and beater often. Pour batter into prepared pans and smooth top with a metal spatula. Bake cake about 25 to 30 minutes, until a toothpick inserted in the center emerges clean. Cool cakes in pan on a rack for 5 minutes, then turn out onto a rack, remove paper, and let cool completely.

# Orange Glaze

**6 tablespoons (½ of a 6-ounce can) frozen**
**orange juice concentrate, thawed**
**3 cups confectioners' sugar, sifted (see Note)**

In a small mixing bowl stir together frozen orange juice concentrate and sugar until smooth. Spread glaze over cooled cake. Store cake in an airtight container.

NOTE: *If you don't have a sifter, you can whisk the sugar for a minute or two.*

*veggie*

# Dump Cake

*Serves 8*

Easy and no mixing bowls to wash!

> *Butter for greasing pan*
> *1 (20-ounce) can crushed pineapple in juice*
> *1 (21-ounce) can cherry pie filling, or a 16-ounce bag*
>   *of frozen filling, thawed*
> *1 box yellow cake mix*
> *4 tablespoons butter*

Preheat oven to 350°F. Grease a 9 × 13-inch baking pan. Spread pineapple on bottom. Spread pie filling evenly over pineapple. Sprinkle the dry cake mix evenly over the pie filling. Cut the butter into small pieces and dot evenly over the cake mix (or melt it and drizzle it). Do not mix! Bake for about 45 to 55 minutes, until the top is golden brown. Remove from oven and allow to cool before cutting into squares. Keep leftover cake cool and dry.

# Chocolate-Peanut Butter Sauce for Ice Cream

*Yields 1 ½ cups*

*¾ cup sugar*

*⅓ cup unsweetened cocoa powder*

*1 (5-ounce) can evaporated milk*

   *(not sweetened condensed)*

*¼ cup chunky peanut butter*

In a small saucepan stir together sugar and cocoa powder. Stir in evaporated milk. Cook and stir over medium-high heat until boiling. Remove from heat. Stir in peanut butter. Serve warm. Store sauce in the refrigerator. Reheat in small saucepan over low heat.

# Quick Banana Dessert

*Serves 1 to 2*

2 bananas, peeled, cut into ½-inch slices
1 tablespoon chopped pecans
3 or 4 heaping tablespoons Cool Whip
   or other frozen dessert topping
¼ teaspoon cinnamon

Gently stir bananas and pecans into topping. Sprinkle with cinnamon and keep chilled until serving.

# Rice Pudding

*Serves 1 to 2*

A great dish to make when you don't know what to do with your leftover rice.

*1 cup cooked rice*

*1 cup milk or heavy cream, or a combination of both*

*3 tablespoons sugar*

*1 tablespoon butter or margarine*

*½ teaspoon vanilla extract*

Combine rice, milk, sugar, and butter in a small saucepan. Cook over medium heat until thickened, about 30 minutes, stirring often. Add vanilla. Pour into serving dish. Serve hot or cold.

*veggie*

# 13.

# HELP!
# A Vegan!

Yes, there *are* delicious and simple animal-friendly choices even carnivores will enjoy!

Vegetarians do not eat fish, poultry, and meat. Vegans, in addition to being vegetarian, do not use other animal products and by-products. A vegan usually abstains from animal products due to ethical reasons; however, some do so for health and environmental motives as well. Many people choose a vegan lifestyle as a way to protest cruel factory-farm conditions as well as to make the choice to contribute to a non-violent, humane world. The practice of veganism entails abstaining from the use of animal products in every aspect of daily life.

You will find many other vegetarian and vegan recipes in this book. The following recipes have been designed for ultimate simplicity. (We're really trying to make this easy for you!)

# Sautéed Summer Vegetable Roll-ups

*Serves 2*

2 tablespoons olive oil

1 medium eggplant, peeled and cubed

1 red bell pepper, cut into strips

4 cloves garlic, peeled and minced

6 ounces (about 1 cup) sliced fresh mushrooms

1 (10-ounce) package frozen chopped spinach,
    thawed and well-drained

6 corn tortillas or pita pockets

Salt and pepper (optional)

Vegan sour cream (optional)

Warm the olive oil over medium heat. Add the eggplant and pepper and sauté until tender but not mushy, about 5 minutes. Add the garlic, mushrooms, and spinach and toss gently about 4 or 5 minutes. If the mixture seems dry, add a little water. Season with salt and pepper, if desired. Fill tortillas and roll up. Top with a dollop of sour cream, if desired.

# Miso Vegetable Soup

*Serves 4*

5 cups water

5 tablespoons miso paste

1 cup cubed tofu

½ cup chopped celery

½ cup chopped carrots

⅓ cup chopped green onions

½ cup snow peas

2 to 4 cloves garlic, peeled

Pour the water into a large soup pot. Over medium heat, dissolve miso paste in water. Add tofu, celery, carrots, green onions, snow peas, and garlic. Simmer on low heat until vegetables are tender, about 10 minutes.

*veggie*

# Creamy Broccoli Soup

*Serves 2*

*Vegetable-oil cooking spray*
*½ medium onion, chopped*
**2 cups canned vegetable broth, or 1 to 2 vegetable bouillon cubes**
 **plus 2 cups water**
*1 cup diced broccoli, cut into small pieces*
*1 tablespoon chopped parsley*
*1 cup soy milk*
*Salt and pepper*

Spray enough vegetable-oil cooking spray into a small skillet to coat the bottom. Over medium heat, sauté onion for 3 minutes. Set aside. In a small saucepan, bring vegetable broth to a boil. Reduce heat; add broccoli and simmer 5 minutes. When slightly cooled, place broth and broccoli in a blender or food processor with sautéed onions and parsley. Blend until smooth. Pour back into saucepan and reheat, adding soy milk just before serving. Add salt and pepper to taste.

# Crunchy Orange-Sesame Salad

*Serves 2*

*1 large cucumber, peeled and thinly sliced*

*1 orange, peeled and sectioned*

*1 to 2 tablespoons chopped peanuts*

*1 tablespoon rice vinegar*

*1 tablespoon sesame oil*

*Salt and pepper*

Combine all ingredients in a serving bowl and keep chilled until ready to serve.

# Black Bean and Toasted Pepita Salad

*Serves 4*

This is wonderful to take to a party.

SALAD

1 (15-ounce) can black beans, rinsed and drained of all liquid

1 cup pepitas (toasted pumpkin seeds)

2 cloves garlic, minced or crushed in garlic press

2 jalapeño peppers, minced

1 red, orange, or yellow bell pepper, chopped

½ of a 10-ounce package frozen petite sweet corn, thawed

1 green onion, sliced thin

Tortilla chips or corn tortillas

MARINADE

3 tablespoons olive or garlic oil

3 tablespoons fresh lime juice

Zest of 1 lime (colored part of skin), minced

1 tablespoon agave nectar (sold in health food stores)

1 teaspoon sweet-and-hot mustard

½ teaspoon ground cumin

2 cloves garlic, minced

Mix all marinade ingredients together in a small glass measuring cup; set aside. Place all salad ingredients except tortilla chips in a large serving bowl. Pour marinade over salad. Toss to mix. Serve with tortilla chips or in warmed soft corn tortillas.

# Confetti Salad

*Serves 2*

1 (15-ounce) can corn, drained of all liquid

1 green pepper, chopped small

1 red, yellow, or orange pepper, chopped small

1 tomato, chopped

¼ cup cider vinegar

2 tablespoons olive oil

Salt and pepper

In a medium serving bowl, combine corn, peppers, and tomato. Toss with vinegar and oil. Add salt and pepper to taste.

# Sweet Potato Casserole Puff

*Serves 2 to 4*

1 (14- or 16-ounce) can sweet potatoes drained of liquid,
   or 2 medium sweet potatoes, baked and cooled
½ of a 14- or 16-ounce package soft tofu (see Note)
¼ cup sugar or maple syrup
2 tablespoons vegetable oil or margarine
½ teaspoon salt
1 teaspoon ground cinnamon
¼ teaspoon ground nutmeg
⅛ teaspoon ground ginger

Preheat oven to 350°F. If using fresh sweet potatoes, scoop pulp out of skins and discard skins. Place all ingredients in a food processor or blender. Blend until smooth. Pour in a greased casserole and bake 40 minutes or until browned around the edges. Serve warm.

NOTE: *You can use the whole package of tofu for a milder flavor.*

# Tofu Dip

*Serves 2 as a main dish, or 4 as an appetizer*

1 (14- or 16-ounce) package firm tofu,
    drained and crumbled
¼ cup eggless mayonnaise
½ teaspoon garlic powder
½ teaspoon onion powder
¼ cup water

Place all the ingredients together in a food processor or blender and blend until creamy. Serve with crackers or crunchy vegetables.

*veggie*

# Tofu Stir-Fry with Peanut Sauce

*Serves 4*

1¾ cups white or brown rice

2 teaspoons peanut oil

1 clove garlic, minced

1 tablespoon minced ginger

1 (16-ounce) package firm or extra-firm tofu,
    drained and diced into small cubes

3 to 4 cups of your favorite vegetables,
    cut up into small pieces

2 tablespoons soy sauce

¼ cup peanut butter

Cook the rice according to the package instructions or microwave (see page 149). Meanwhile, heat oil in a wok or large skillet over medium heat. Add the garlic and ginger, stirring until they begin to soften, about 2 minutes. Add the tofu and vegetables, stir, cover, and cook for 5 minutes.

Gently mix the vegetables and tofu. Add 2 tablespoons of water if the mixture seems dry, and replace cover. Repeat every 5 minutes until the vegetables are crisp-firm, about 15 minutes. Add soy sauce and toss.

Add 1 teaspoon of water to peanut butter and mix until well combined. Continue to add water, 1 teaspoon at a time, until peanut sauce can be poured. Serve the stir-fry over the cooked rice with peanut sauce poured on top.

# The Vegan Triple Decker Club Sandwich

*Serves 1*

3 slices whole-wheat or other whole-grain bread

½ *small cucumber, peeled and thinly sliced*

½ *cup alfalfa sprouts*

½ *tomato, thinly sliced*

1 avocado, peeled, seeded, and sliced

2 lettuce leaves

1 tablespoon eggless mayonnaise

Toast bread. Top one slice with half of all ingredients. Top with another toast slice and remaining ingredients. Top with third slice. Cut sandwich into quarters.

*veggie*

# Fried Portobello "Steak" Sandwiches

*Serves 2*

For an even heartier sandwich, add some grilled eggplant and/or roasted red bell peppers.

*2 tablespoons olive oil*

*1 clove garlic, minced*

*2 portobella mushroom caps (remove stems), sliced*

*4 slices whole-wheat bread*

*2 large lettuce or spinach leaves*

In a large skillet, heat olive oil over medium heat. Add garlic and sauté for 2 to 3 minutes. Add mushrooms and sauté until heated through, about 3 minutes on each side. Toast bread. Divide mushrooms into even servings, and assemble sandwiches.

# Stuffed Peppers

*Serves 2*

*2 large green peppers, tops and seeds removed*

*2 teaspoons vegetable oil*

*1 small onion, chopped*

*1 (14-ounce) package soy protein "ground meat,"*
  *thawed if frozen*

*1 tomato, chopped*

*Salt and pepper*

Bring a large pot of water to a boil. Submerge peppers and boil for 10 minutes. Carefully remove peppers with tongs and drain. In a medium saucepan or skillet, heat oil over medium low heat and sauté onion until lightly browned, add soy protein until heated through. Add tomato and stir mixture for about 1 minute. Remove from heat and add salt and pepper to taste. Stuff peppers and serve.

*veggie*

# Hummus

*Serves 2*

1 (15-ounce) can garbanzo beans (chickpeas),
    drained of all liquid
¼ cup tahini (sesame paste)
2 teaspoons sesame oil
1 tablespoon lemon juice
2 to 4 cloves garlic, minced
¼ teaspoon salt
¼ to ½ teaspoon cayenne (optional)

Process all ingredients in a blender until smooth. Serve with pita bread wedges. You could also serve hummus with pita crisps, bagel chips, rye toast, carrot sticks, or celery sticks.

# Oatmeal and Fruit Bar Cookies

*Yields about 1 dozen cookies*

*2 large ripe bananas, peeled and mashed*

*2 cups quick-cooking rolled oats*

*1 cup shredded coconut*

*¼ cup maple syrup*

*Vegetable-oil spray for greasing baking pan*

Preheat oven to 350°F. Mix ingredients together in a large bowl. Press mixture into a greased baking pan. Bake for 30 minutes. Remove from oven and allow to cool before slicing. Slice into 12 bars.

# Vegan Chocolate Pudding

1½ *cups crumbled silken tofu, drained*

⅔ *cup unbleached cane sugar*

⅓ *cup unsweetened cocoa powder*

2 *teaspoons vanilla extract*

**Pinch of salt**

Blend all ingredients together in a blender or food processor. Chill until firm. Spoon into serving glasses.

# 14.

# You're on Your Way to Becoming a Gourmet!

## THREE TIPS FOR THROWING A VERY SIMPLE DINNER PARTY

- It's best to keep things intimate—four to six people total is best, maybe a few more if your place can handle it.
- Have you perfected one great recipe? Make that, and ask your guests to bring a side dish.
- Since you're making the effort, make it special. Fresh flowers, a nice tablecloth, candles, and appropriate music will add a lot of atmosphere.

*veggie*

# Waldorf Salad

*Serves 2*

This colorful, crunchy salad has a reputation as being fancy and gourmet, but it's really easy to make.

> 2 red apples, chopped into bite-sized pieces
>
> 2 tablespoons orange juice
>
> 2 stalks celery, chopped into bite-sized pieces
>
> ½ cup chopped walnuts
>
> ½ cup raisins
>
> ¼ cup mayonnaise

Place chopped apples in a small bowl and add orange juice. (This keeps the apples from turning brown.) In a larger bowl, combine remaining ingredients. Add apples and mix well. Keep chilled until ready to eat.

# Cheese Soufflé

*Serves 2 to 4*

Forget all those horror stories you've heard about soufflés. This one is simple, foolproof, and very hearty.

*1½ cups (6 ounces) shredded jack cheese*

*½ cup Bisquick or other biscuit mix*

*¼ cup milk*

*3 eggs*

*3 tablespoons butter or margarine, room temperature*

*3 tablespoons cottage cheese*

*Butter for greasing casserole*

*1 tablespoon chopped chives or green onions (optional)*

Preheat oven to 350°F. In a medium mixing bowl, beat all ingredients together with an electric mixer. Pour into greased 1-quart casserole or baking dish with high sides. Bake 30 to 40 minutes or until light brown. Serve with any favorite salad.

# Cheesy Stuffed Chicken

*Serves 6*

**6 skinless, boneless chicken breast halves**
**½ teaspoon salt**
**½ teaspoon black pepper**
**4 ounces pepper jack cheese, cut into 6 chunks**
**Vegetable-oil cooking spray, for greasing muffin tin cups**
**1 tablespoon seasoned bread crumbs**
**⅛ teaspoon paprika**

Preheat oven to 350°F. Between 2 pieces of wax paper, gently pound the chicken to ¼-inch thickness with a mallet or rolling pin. Sprinkle both sides of each breast lightly with the salt and pepper then place a cheese chunk in the center of each piece of chicken and roll each breast tightly, tucking in the sides as you roll. Place the rolls seam side down in greased medium muffin tin cups. Mix the bread crumbs and paprika in a small bowl. Sprinkle ½ teaspoon of the seasoned breadcrumbs over each roll. Bake for 25 to 30 minutes, or until no pink remains and the juices run clear. Serve immediately. Serve with a tossed green salad.

# Broiled Steak, Gourmet-Style

*Serves 2*

2 steaks, 8 to 10 ounces each, Porterhouse, strip,
  or any other you prefer
2 tablespoons mayonnaise
1 tablespoon Dijon mustard
1 teaspoon dried tarragon (optional)
½ teaspoon garlic powder
¼ teaspoon salt
¼ teaspoon black pepper

Preheat the broiler and broiling pan on high for about 5 minutes. (For best results, use a pan and rack combination especially designed for broiling.) Place the steaks on a large platter. In a small bowl, combine the remaining ingredients; mix well. Spread the mixture over the steaks, coating well. Place the steaks on the heated broiler rack. Broil for 10 to 12 minutes for medium-rare, or to desired doneness beyond that, turning with tongs halfway through the cooking. Serve with French-Style Potatoes (page 161) and Baked Green Beans (page 163).

*veggie*

# Gourmet Cucumbers

*Serves 1 to 2*

1 cucumber, peeled and thinly sliced

1 small onion, sliced into thin rings

2 tablespoons sugar

2 tablespoons vegetable oil

1 tablespoon rice or white vinegar

¼ teaspoon salt

⅓ cup sour cream or unflavored yogurt

1 tablespoon chopped chives or parsley (optional)

Place cucumber and onion slices in salad bowl. In a small mixing bowl, combine sugar, oil and vinegar, and salt. Pour over cucumber. Marinate 20 minutes, tossing occasionally to distribute marinade. Drain marinade from cucumbers. Stir in sour cream and top with chives, if using. Best if refrigerated overnight.

# CHEESE FONDUE

Fondue is excellent for taking the chill out of winter. Legend has it that fondue was created by a shepherd in the Swiss Alps who was inspired to heat his nightly dinner of wine and cheese in a pot, then scoop out the delicious concoction with chunks of crusty bread.

For those of you who have never tried making this indulgent dish, you'll be delightfully surprised at how easy it is. If you can grate cheese and stir with a wooden spoon, you will have mastered the fondue. It's that easy!

Fondue is the perfect party dish. Guests spear a cube of bread, dip it in the hot cheese, swirl it around, and eat.

## Popular cheeses for fondue include:

- **Emmentaler:** Switzerland's oldest cheese, it has a distinctly nutty-sweet, mellow flavor. It has a pale yellow interior with a light brown rind.
- **Gruyère:** This Swiss cheese has a rich, sweet, nutty flavor with a pale yellow interior and a golden brown rind. It has a stronger flavor than Emmentaler.
- **Camembert:** This cheese has an edible, downy white rind and a smooth, creamy interior with an aromatic flavor. Select cheese that is plump and soft to the touch, but not runny.
- **Brie:** This cheese has an edible, downy white rind and a cream-colored interior. Look for Brie that is plump and resilient to the touch.
- **Feta:** This cheese is white and crumbly with a sharp and pungent flavor.
- **Other cheeses** such as cheddar or jack can be mixed in with the more traditional Swiss.

## Fondue tips:

- **You may cook the fondue** in a heavy saucepan first, transferring to the fondue pot once all the cheese has melted. The gentle flame under the fondue pot will maintain a lower heat needed to prevent scorching. Beforehand, you may wish to warm the fondue pot by using boiling water as a "stand in" for the cheese mixture.
- **Add the cheese in small handfuls** and stir constantly for a smooth fondue.
- **If the fondue becomes too thick** during stovetop cooking or while in the fondue pot,

gradually whisk in a few tablespoons of brandy that has first been brought to a simmer. Repeat this step as needed.

- **When you reach the end of the pot,** you'll find thick grilled cheese at the bottom. This is a rich, delicious, highly prized delicacy, and should be shared.
- **What to do with leftover cheese fondue?** It can be used as a savory topping for rice or baked potatoes, or as a filling for omelets.

# Cheese Fondue

*Serves 4*

*4 ounces Gruyère cheese*
*8 ounces Swiss cheese*
*1 tablespoon cornstarch*
*1 clove garlic*
*1 cup dry white wine*
*Freshly grated nutmeg*
*Freshly ground pepper*
*Crusty French bread cut into 1-inch cubes*
*Sliced apples and pears*

Grate cheese and mix with cornstarch. Cut garlic clove in half. Rub garlic over inside of fondue pot. Mince the other half-clove and add to pot. Add wine to pot and heat slowly until it just bubbles. Slowly add the cheese mixture, stirring as it melts. When smooth, add nutmeg and pepper. Serve with French bread and sliced fruit.

*veggie*

# Camembert and Apple Fondue

Crisp apples, cored, peeled, and cut into chunks, should be prepared at the last moment to ensure that they do not turn brown.

*½ clove garlic*

*1 cup light cream or half-and-half*

*2½ cups (about 10 ounces) cubed Camembert*

*1 tablespoon cornstarch*

*3 tablespoons apple cider or apple brandy*

*2 or 3 large apples, cut into bite-sized chunks*

*Lemon juice*

Rub the inside of a fondue pot with the cut garlic. Heat the fondue pot on medium. Add the cream and cheese. Stir while the cheese melts. Blend the cornstarch with the apple cider. Stir into the cheese mixture and cook for 2 minutes, stirring. Put the apple chunks in a bowl and coat with lemon juice. Pat dry on paper towels. Serve fondue with apple chunks.

# Glossary of Cooking Terms

**Bake**—To cook in an oven using dry heat

**Baste**—To moisten food while cooking by pouring or spooning over pan juices or sauce

**Batter**—A liquid mix of ingredients, usually containing flour and eggs

**Beat**—To use a fork, spoon, whisk, etc. to incorporate air into a mixture while mixing ingredients together

**Blend**—To mix two or more ingredients together until smooth

**Boil**—To heat liquid until bubbles break the surface

**Broil**—To cook with direct intense heat under the broiler unit of an oven, usually no more than 5 inches from the heat source

**Brown**—To cook quickly at a high temperature until color changes to light brown

**Butter**—To rub butter, oil, or shortening inside a pan so food will not stick. Also known as "grease"

**Chill**—To refrigerate until cold

**Chop**—The general term for cutting things into pieces

**Cream**—To beat until soft and creamy, usually mixing butter with sugar

**Crisp**—Achieving a crisp outer shell on food by heating

**Dash**—To add a very small amount, between $\frac{1}{16}$ and $\frac{1}{8}$ teaspoon

**Dice**—To cut into very small squares

**Dot**—To put small pieces of butter here and there on top of food

**Dust**—To lightly coat a food with either flour or confectioners' sugar

**Flake**—To shave or chip off small layers

**Fold**—To mix very gently, by bringing spoon or spatula down, up, and over, without losing air or volume

**Fry**—To cook food in hot oil or butter in a skillet, usually forming crisp outer crust

**Garlic clove**—One small section of a whole garlic head

**Garlic head**—The whole garlic bulb, made up of small sections of cloves

**Garnish**—To decorate food with colorful additions such as parsley

**Grease**—See Butter

**Marinate**—To allow food to soak in a seasoned mixture, adding flavor and making the food tender

**Mince**—To chop or cut into very tiny pieces

**Parboil**—To precook a food by boiling in water

**Pinch**—The small amount of a dry ingredient that you can hold between your thumb and forefinger

**Preheat**—To heat an oven or pan to the desired temperature before adding food

**Sauté**—To cook or fry in a small amount of oil

**Separate (eggs)**—To "separate" the yolk from the whites by gently cracking the egg and pouring the egg back and forth between the two shell halves, allowing the whites to collect in a bowl and leaving the yolk in the shell

**Shred**—To cut into very thin, long, narrow strips

**Simmer**—To cook in a liquid that is almost boiling but not bubbling

**Stiff peaks**—Egg whites that have been whipped or beaten until high in volume so they hold their "peaks"

**Toss**—To mix together lightly

**Whisk**—To beat lightly and quickly. Also, the utensil, consisting of several loops of wire attached to a handle

**Zest**—The colored outer skin of a citrus fruit, minced or grated (the white pith, underneath, is bitter and generally avoided in cooking)

# Food Storage Index

As a general rule, **the fresher the food, the faster it will spoil**. A sun-ripened peach won't last a day sitting out on the counter in your dorm room; however, white rice and white sugar will keep almost indefinitely on the pantry shelf. (Although once opened, they should be stored in tightly-closed containers to keep out varmints, dust, moisture, and other contaminants.) Brown rice, because of the oil in the bran layer, and brown sugar, because of its high molasses content, both have much shorter shelf lives.

Toss out food that seems bad. Beware of bread with green spots, fruit turning spongy or squashy, vegetables growing fuzz, and raw meat that has turned dark.

If you are ever in doubt whether a food item should go in the pantry or the refrigerator, it's best to keep it in the refrigerator. Some pantry items do much better chilled (bread, rice cakes, chips) when the weather is warm or muggy.

Store leftovers in see-through containers to avoid nasty surprises.

# From the Bakery

| ITEM | SHELF | REFRIGERATOR | FREEZER |
|------|-------|--------------|---------|
| Bread, commercial | 2 to 4 days | 7 to 14 days | 3 months |
| Bread, flat (tortillas, pita) | 2 to 4 days | 4 to 7 days | 4 months |
| Cake, Angel Food* | 1 to 2 days | 7 days | 2 months |
| Cake, chiffon, sponge | 1 to 2 days | 7 days | 2 months |
| Cake, chocolate | 1 to 2 days | 7 days | 4 months |
| Cake, fruit cake | 1 month | 6 months | 12 months |
| Cake, made from mix | 3 to 4 days | 7 days | 4 months |
| Cake, pound cake | 3 to 4 days | 7 days | 6 months |
| Cheesecake | No | 7 days | 2 to 3 months |
| Cookies, bakery or homemade | 2 to 3 weeks | 2 months | 8 to 12 months |
| Croissants, butter | 1 day | 7 days | 2 months |
| Doughnuts, dairy cream-filled | No | 3 to 4 days | No |
| Doughnuts, glazed or cake | 1 to 2 days | 7 days | 1 month |
| Muffins | No | 3 to 4 days | No |
| Pastries, Danish | 1 to 2 days | 7 days | 2 months |
| Pie, chiffon | No | 1 to 2 days | No |
| Pie, cream | No | 3 to 4 days | 2 months |
| Pie, filled, meat or vegetables | 2 hours | 3 to 4 days | 2 monthsPie, |
| Pie, fruit | 1 to 2 days | 7 days | No |
| Pie, mincemeat | 1 to 2 days | 7 days | 8 months |
| Pie, pecan | 2 hours | 3 to 4 days | 8 months |
| Pie, pumpkin | 2 hours | 3 to 4 days | 1–2 months |
| Quiche | 3 to 4 days | 7 days | 1–2 months |
| Rolls, yeast, baked | Package date | 7 days | 2 months |

*Refrigerate any cake with frosting made of cream cheese, butter cream, whipped cream, or eggs.

# SHELF-STABLE FOODS

Most unopened shelf-stable food should be stored in a cool, dry, and dark storage area.

Before opening, shelf-stable foods should be safe unless the can or packaging has been damaged. After opening, store products in tightly closed containers.

The storage of many shelf-stable items at room temperature is not a quality issue unless the product is contaminated (bugs in flour, for example).

Some foods must be refrigerated after opening, such as tuna or chili. Canned foods should be transfered to a glass or plastic container. Do not store in can.

| BABY FOOD JARS AND CANS | UNOPENED | OPEN REFRIGERATED | OPEN ON SHELF |
|---|---|---|---|
| Cereal, dry mixes | Use-by date | | 2 months |
| Formula | Use-by date | 1 to 2 days | |
| Fruits and vegetables | 2 months after date | 2 to 3 days | No |
| Meats and eggs | 2 months after date | 1 day | No |

| BAKING INGREDIENTS | UNOPENED | OPEN REFRIGERATED | OPEN ON SHELF |
|---|---|---|---|
| Baking powder | 6 months | 6 months | 3 months |
| Baking soda | 18 months | 6 months | 6 months |
| Biscuit or pancake mix | 15 months | Use-by date | Use-by date |
| Cake, brownie and bread mixes | 12 to 18 months | Use-by date | Use-by date |
| Cornmeal, regular, degerminated | 6 to 12 months | 12 months | Use-by date |
| Cornmeal, stone-ground or blue | 1 month | 2 to 3 months | Use-by date |
| Cornstarch | 18 months | 18 months | 18 months |
| Flour, white (all-purpose) | 6 to 12 months | 6 to 12 months | 6 to 8 months |
| Flour, whole-wheat | 1 month | 6 to 8 months | Use-by date |

*(continued)*

## SHELF-STABLE ITEMS *(continued)*

| BAKING INGREDIENTS | UNOPENED | OPENED REFRIGERATED | OPEN ON SHELF |
|---|---|---|---|
| Frosting, canned | 10 months | 1 week | Not recommended |
| Frosting, mixes | 12 months | 1 month | 3 months |
| Chocolate | 18 to 24 months | Not recommended | 1 year |
| Chocolate syrup | 2 years | 6 months | Not recommended |
| Cocoa and cocoa mixes | indefinitely | 1 year | 1 year |
| Shortening, solid | 8 months | 8 months | 8 months |

| COFFEE | UNOPENED | OPEN REFRIGERATED | OPEN ON SHELF |
|---|---|---|---|
| Whole beans, non-vacuum bag | 1 to 3 weeks | 3 to 4 months frozen | Not recommended |
| Ground, in cans | 2 years | 2 weeks | Not recommended |
| Instant, jars and tins | 12 months | 2 to 3 months | 2 to 3 months |

# SHELF-STABLE ITEMS *(continued)*

| SAVORY CONDIMENTS | UNOPENED | OPEN REFRIGERATED | OPEN ON SHELF |
|---|---|---|---|
| Barbecue sauce, bottled | 12 months | 4 months | 1 month |
| Horseradish, in jar | 12 months | 3 to 4 months | Not recommended |
| Ketchup, tomato; cocktail sauce or chili sauce | 12 months | 6 months | 1 month |
| Mayonnaise, commercial | 2 to 3 months | 2 months | Not recommended |
| Olives, black and green | 12 to 18 months | 2 weeks | Not recommended |
| Pickles | 12 months | 1 to 2 months | Not recommended |
| Salad dressings, commercial, bottled | 10 to 12 months | 3 months | Not recommended |
| Salsa; picante and taco sauces | 12 months | 1 month | Not recommended |
| Garlic, chopped, commercial jars | 18 months | Refrigerate, use-by date on jar | Not recommended |
| Gravy, jars and cans | 2 to 5 years | 1 to 2 days | Not recommended |
| Herbs, dried | 1 to 2 years | Not recommended | Store in a cool dark place 1 year |

# SHELF-STABLE ITEMS *(continued)*

| SWEET CONDIMENTS | UNOPENED | OPEN REFRIGERATED | OPEN ON SHELF |
|---|---|---|---|
| Honey | 12 months | Not recommended | 12 months |
| Jams, jellies, preserves | 12 months | 6 months | Not recommended |
| Juice boxes | 4 to 6 months | 8 to 12 days | Not recommended |
| Marshmallows, marshmallow creme | 2 to 4 months | 2 to 4 months | 1 month |
| Milk, canned evaporated | 12 months | 4 to 5 days | Not recommended |
| Molasses | 12 months | 12 months | 6 months |
| Peanut butter, commercial | 6 to 9 months | 6 months | 2 to 3 months |
| Sugar, brown | Indefinitely | Not recommended | 1 year |
| Sugar, confectioners' | 18 months | 18 months | 1 year |
| Sugar, granulated | Indefinitely | Indefinitely | Indefinitely |
| Syrup, pancake, maple | 12 months | 12 months | 12 months |

| STARCHES | UNOPENED | OPEN REFRIGERATED | OPEN ON SHELF |
|---|---|---|---|
| Pasta, dry, made without eggs | 2 years | 6 months | 1 year |
| Pasta, dry egg noodles | 2 years | 6 months | 1 to 2 months |
| Popcorn, dry kernels in jar | 2 years | 1 year | 1 year |
| Potato chips | 2 months | 2 months | 1 to 2 weeks |
| Potatoes, instant mashed | 6 to 12 months | 6 to 12 months | 6 to 12 months |
| Ramen | 12 months | 6 months | Not recommended |
| Rice, brown | 1 year | 6 months | 1 year |
| Rice, white or wild | 2 years | 1 year | 1 year |
| Rice, flavored or herb mixes | 6 months | | Use entire package |

| FROZEN ITEM | FREEZER | IN REFRIGERATOR AFTER THAWING |
|---|---|---|
| Bagels | 2 months | 1 to 2 weeks |
| Bread dough, commercial | Use-by date | After baking, 4 to 7 days |
| Burritos, sandwiches | 2 months | 3 to 4 days |
| Egg substitutes | 12 months | Date on carton |
| Fish, breaded | 3 months | Do not thaw. Cook frozen. |
| Fish, raw | 6 months | 1 day |
| Fruit such as berries, melons | 4 to 6 months | 4 to 5 days |
| Guacamole | 3 to 4 months | 3 to 4 days |
| Ice cream | 2 to 4 months | Not applicable |
| Juice concentrates | 6 to 12 months | 7 to 10 days |
| Lobster tails | 3 months | 2 days |
| Pancakes, waffles | 2 months | 3 to 4 days |
| Sausages, precooked | 1 to 2 months | 7 days |
| Sausages, uncooked | 1 to 2 months | 1 to 2 days |
| Sherbet, sorbet | 2 to 4 months | Not applicable |
| Shrimp, shellfish | 12 months | 1 day |
| Topping, whipped | 6 months | 2 weeks |
| TV dinners, entrees, breakfast | 3 months | Do not defrost. Cook frozen. |
| Vegetables | 8 months | 3 to 4 days |

# STORING FRUITS AND VEGETABLES

Raw fruits are safe at room temperature, but after ripening, will mold and rot quickly. For best quality, store ripe fruit in the refrigerator or prepare and freeze.

This chart assumes that you are buying your fruit in a retail store. Shelf life will increase dramatically if you are able to buy your produce directly from the source. For example, assuming you have the proper storage area and are able to buy your apples during harvest, they will easily last for 6 months or longer.

| FRESH FRUIT | SHELF | REFRIGERATOR | FREEZER |
|---|---|---|---|
| Apples | 1 to 2 days | 3 weeks | Cooked, 8 months |
| Apricots | Until ripe | 2 to 3 days | Halves, 8 months |
| Avocados | Until ripe | 3 to 4 days | No |
| Bananas | Until ripe | 2 days, skin will blacken | whole peeled, 1 month |
| Berries, cherries | No | 1 to 2 days | 4 months |
| Citrus fruit | 10 days | 1 to 2 weeks | No |
| Coconuts, fruits | 1 week | 2 to 3 weeks | Shredded, 6 months |
| Grapes | 1 day | 1 week | Whole, 1 month |
| Kiwi fruit | Until ripe | 3 to 4 days | No |
| Melons | 1 to 2 days | 3 to 4 days | Balls, 1 month |
| Papaya, mango | 3 to 5 days | 1 week | Sliced, 8 months |
| Peaches, nectarines | Until ripe | 3 to 4 days | Sliced, 8 months |
| Pears | 3 to 5 days | 3 to 4 days | No |
| Plums | 3 to 5 days | 3 to 4 days | Halves, 8 months |

| FRESH VEGETABLE | SHELF | RAW, REFRIGERATED | BLANCHED OR COOKED, FROZEN |
|---|---|---|---|
| Artichokes, whole | 1 to 2 days | 1 to 2 weeks | No |
| Asparagus | No | 3 to 4 days | 8 months |

(continued)

# STORING FRUITS AND VEGETABLES *(continued)*

| FRESH VEGETABLE | SHELF | RAW, REFRIGERATED | BLANCHED OR COOKED, FROZEN |
|---|---|---|---|
| Beans, green or wax | No | 3 to 4 days | 8 months |
| Beets | 1 day | 7 to 10 days | 6 to 8 months |
| Cabbage | No | 1 to 2 weeks | 10 to 12 months |
| Carrots, parsnips | No | 2 weeks | 10 to 12 months |
| Celery | No | 1 to 2 weeks | 10 to 12 months |
| Cucumbers | No | 4 to 5 days | No |
| Eggplant | 1 day | 3 to 4 days | 6 to 8 months |
| Garlic, ginger root | 2 days | 1 to 2 weeks | 1 month |
| Greens | No | 1 to 2 days | 10 to 12 months |
| Herbs, fresh | No | 7 to 10 days | 1 to 2 months |
| Leeks | No | 1 to 2 weeks | 10 to 12 months |
| Lettuce, iceberg | No | 1 to 2 weeks | No |
| Lettuce, leaf | No | 3 to 7 days | No |
| Mushrooms | No | 2 to 3 days | 10 to 12 months |
| Okra | No | 2 to 3 days | 10 to 12 months |
| Onions, dry | 2 to 3 weeks | 2 months | 10 to 12 months |
| Onions (spring or green scallions) | No | 1 to 2 weeks | |
| Peppers, bell or chili | No | 4 to 5 days | 6 to 8 months |
| Potatoes | 1 to 2 months | 1 to 2 weeks | Cooked and mashed, 10 to 12 months |
| Rutabagas | 1 week | 2 weeks | 8 to 10 months |
| Spinach | No | 1 to 2 days | 10 to 12 months |
| Squash, summer | No | 4 to 5 days | 10 to 12 months |
| Squash, winter | 1 week | 2 weeks | |
| Tomatoes | Until ripe | 2 to 3 days | 2 months |
| Turnips | No | 2 weeks | 8 to 10 months |

# Have You Checked Your Refrigerator Lately?

| PRODUCT | REFRIGERATED | FROZEN |
|---|---|---|
| **Beverages** | | |
| Fruit | 3 weeks unopened | |
| Juice in cartons, fruit drinks, punch | 7 to 10 days open | 8 to 12 months |
| | | |
| **Condiments** | | |
| Refrigerated pesto, salsa | Date on carton; 3 days after opening | 1 to 2 months |
| Sour cream-based dip | 2 weeks | Do not freeze |
| | | |
| **Dairy products** | | |
| Butter | 1 to 3 months | 6 to 9 months |
| Buttermilk | 7 to 14 days | 3 months |
| Cheese, hard (cheddar, Swiss) | 6 months unopened; 3 to 4 weeks opened | 6 months |
| Cheese, soft (Brie, Bel Paese) | 1 week | 6 months |
| Cottage cheese, ricotta | 1 week | Do not freeze |
| Cream cheese | 2 weeks | Do not freeze |
| Cream, aerosol can, nondairy | 3 months | Do not freeze |
| Cream, aerosol can, real whipped | 3 to 4 weeks | Do not freeze |
| Cream, half-and-half | 3 to 4 days | 4 months |
| Cream, heavy, ultrapasteurized | 1 month | Do not freeze |
| Cream, whipped, sweetened | 1 day | 1 to 2 months |
| Margarine | 4 to 5 months | 12 months |
| Milk | 7 days | 3 months |
| Pudding | Package date; 2 days after opening | Do not freeze |
| Sour cream | 1 to 3 weeks | Do not freeze |
| Yogurt | 1 to 2 weeks | 1 to 2 months |

*(continued)*

| PRODUCT | REFRIGERATED | FROZEN |
| --- | --- | --- |
| **Deli foods** | | |
| Entrees, cold or hot | 3 to 4 days | 2 to 3 months |
| Lunch meats, store-sliced | 3 to 5 days | 1 to 2 months |
| Salads | 3 to 5 days | Do not freeze |
| | | |
| **Dough** | | |
| Cookie dough | Use-by date | 2 months |
| Ready-to-bake pie crust | Use-by date | 2 months |
| Tube cans of biscuits, rolls, pizza dough, etc. | Use-by date | Do not freeze |
| | | |
| **Eggs** | | |
| Eggnog, commercial | 3 to 5 days | 6 months |
| Eggs, in shell | 3 to 5 weeks | Do not freeze |
| Hard-boiled | 1 week | Do not freeze |
| Raw whites | 2 to 4 days | 12 months |
| Raw yolks | 2 to 4 days | Do not freeze |
| Substitutes, liquid, opened | 3 days | Do not freeze |
| Substitutes, liquid, unopened | 10 days | Do not freeze |
| | | |
| **Fish** | | |
| Caviar, fresh, nonpasteurized | 6 months unopened; 2 days after opening | Do not freeze |
| Caviar, pasteurized, vacuum-packaged | 1 year unopened 2 days after opening | Do not freeze |
| Cooked fish | 3 to 4 days | 4 to 6 months |
| Fatty fish (bluefish, mackerel, salmon, etc.) | 1 to 2 days | 2 to 3 months |

*(continued)*

| PRODUCT | REFRIGERATED | FROZEN |
| --- | --- | --- |
| Lean fish (cod, flounder, haddock, sole, etc.) | 1 to 2 days | 6 months |
| Smoked fish | 14 days or date on package | 2 months in vacuum package |
| **Shellfish** | | |
| Cooked shellfish | 3 to 4 days | 3 months |
| Live clams, mussels, crab, lobster, and oysters | 2 to 3 days | 2 to 3 months |
| Shrimp, scallops, crayfish, squid | 1 to 2 days | 3 to 6 months |
| Shucked clams, mussels, oysters | 1 to 2 days | 3 to 6 months |
| **Meat, fresh** | | |
| Beef, lamb, pork, or veal chops, steaks, roasts | 3 to 5 days | 4 to 12 months |
| Cooked meats (home cooked) | 3 to 4 days | 2 to 3 months |
| Ground meat | 1 to 2 days | 3 to 4 months |
| Variety meats (liver, tongue, chitterlings, etc.) | 1 to 2 days | 3 to 4 months |
| **Meat, smoked or processed** | | |
| Bacon | 7 days | 1 month |
| Corned beef, in pouch with juices | 5 to 7 days | 1 month |
| Ham, canned ("keep refrigerated" label) | 6 to 9 months | Do not freeze |
| Ham, fully cooked, slices or halves | 3 to 4 days | 1 to 2 months |

*(continued)*

| PRODUCT | REFRIGERATED | FROZEN |
| --- | --- | --- |
| Ham, fully cooked, whole | 7 days | 1 to 2 months |
| Hot dogs, after opening | 1 week | 1 to 2 months |
| Hot dogs, sealed in package | 2 weeks | 1 to 2 months |
| Lunch meats, after opening | 3 to 5 days | 1 to 2 months |
| Lunch meats, sealed in package | 2 weeks | 1 to 2 months |
| Pasta, fresh | 1 to 2 days or package date | 2 months |
| Sausage, hard, dry (pepperoni), sliced | 2 to 3 weeks | 1 to 2 months |
| Sausage, raw, bulk type | 1 to 2 days | 1 to 2 months |
| Sausage, smoked links, patties | 7 days | 1 to 2 months |
| **Poultry, fresh** | | |
| Chicken or turkey, parts | 1 to 2 days | 9 months |
| Chicken or turkey, whole | 1 to 2 days | 12 months |
| Duckling or goose, whole | 1 to 2 days | 6 months |
| Giblets | 1 to 2 days | 3 to 4 months |
| **Poultry, cooked or processed** | | |
| Chicken nuggets, patties | 1 to 2 days | 1 to 3 months |
| Cooked poultry dishes | 3 to 4 days | 4 to 6 months |
| Fried chicken | 3 to 4 days | 4 months |
| Ground turkey or chicken | 1 to 2 days | 3 to 4 months |
| Lunch meats, sealed in package | 2 weeks | 1 to 2 months |
| Lunch meats, after opening | 3 to 5 days | 1 to 2 months |
| Pieces covered with broth or gravy | 1 to 2 days | 6 months |
| Rotisserie chicken | 3 to 4 days | 4 months |

# Index